The School Library:
Responding to Change

Resources in Education

Other titles in this series:

The School Library
Responding to Change

Elizabeth King
MA ALA

Past Chairperson of the
School Library Association

Northcote House

This book is dedicated to the memory of my parents, Jack and
Agnes Fordham. Dedicated teachers both, they had a great
love of reading and of the power of education to transform
people's lives. They gave me, and their pupils, their own love
of literature and learning, and so their influence lives on.

British Library Cataloguing in Publication Data
King, Elizabeth, 1934 –
    The school library: responding to change. –
    (Resources in education series).
    1. Great Britain.   Schools.   Libraries
    I. Title II. Series
    027.8′0941

    ISBN 0-7463-0517-6

First published in 1989 by Northcote House Publishers Ltd,
Harper & Row House, Estover Road, Plymouth PL6 7PZ,
United Kingdom. Tel: Plymouth (0752) 705251.
Telex: 45635. Fax: (0752) 777603.

Typesetting and Artwork by K-Dee Typesetters.

Printed in Great Britain by A. Wheaton & Co., Ltd., Exeter

Preface

This book is aimed primarily at the education world and is particularly appropriate for those teachers already working in school libraries, those interested in this area of work and those involved in training school librarians. It is not wholly a library skills manual, although useful guidelines and ideas will be found to help with library routines. More, it aims to put the school library into an educational perspective, to draw the threads together which have led to the present situation and to examine how best to move forwards.

Contents

1
The Resource Implications of Educational Change

'The school library becomes a force for educational excellence when it functions as an integral part of the total educational programme.' So said Ruth Davies in her powerfully argued book *The School Library*.

The traditional role of the school library has always been to support the educational work of the school and to supply all the essential resources to fulfil that aim. In spite of all the many and varied upheavals in the educational world over the last twenty or so years, that basic premise has not altered. Any library, whether in a school or not, that attempts to work in isolation from the real needs of its clientele is doomed to failure, and only an active, participative and responsive service can, or indeed should, survive.

Educational libraries have had to learn to adapt to all sorts of changes, not only in the educational structure, in different teaching methods (and, by implication, in the resources and materials needed), but also to new subjects, new technologies and a bewildering variety of educational initiatives. Much of this has had to be accomplished with no extra money and, in fact, often a real and substantial cut in finance. Poor staffing, particularly in terms of time allowed for the library and in the availability and access to appropriate in-service training, has exacerbated an already difficult situation.

Coupled with these fundamental changes in the face of education, there has also been an increasing pressure from pupils, teachers, examination boards and parents to ensure that all the necessary materials are provided for all ages and abilities—albeit with little or no extra finance. As the role of the teacher has gradually moved from that of a deliverer of information to one more concerned with the facilitating of independent learning on the part of the pupil, so not only have teaching strategies altered but a much wider variety of resources has been needed to support this changed emphasis. To respond to the demands of education in the latter part of the 1980s has not been easy for any teacher but much of the pressure has fallen on school librarians and on their ability not only to support, but also extend, the curriculum.

The changes in education which have directly influenced the role of the school library may be divided into three main categories:
1. Structural and managerial change;
2. Curriculum development;
3. Impact of new technologies.

STRUCTURAL AND MANAGERIAL CHANGE

Most areas of the country have been through a radical process of change during the last twenty to thirty years, but the one to have probably had the largest impact on both teachers and resources has been the emergence of the comprehensive school, coupled with the disappearance of the old grammar school/secondary modern split. This move involved all secondary schools in upheaval to some degree or another but, perhaps as important as the structural change, it also resulted in a change in both educational philosophy and educational sociology by placing more emphasis on individual achievement. Additionally, it had a profound effect on both the curriculum and on teaching methods: new subjects were introduced and some of the more traditional grammar school subjects like Greek largely faded out to be replaced by more vocational subjects such as business studies or craft.

As a direct result of this change to comprehensive education, most high schools became much bigger and many schools amalgamated. The school library that had been adequate for a small school with a relatively even spread of ability and a staff that largely knew all the pupils and each other proved to be totally ineffective in schools having anything up to 2,000 pupils, often on a split site, and with students whose intelligence ranged from potential Oxbridge to near illiterate. Resource provision had to expand very quickly to cope, but this explosion of material into schools also called for a much more structured and organised approach to the school library than had been necessary before. Unfortunately, this did not always figure high on the head's priority list and many schools still suffer from the deficiencies in library organisation ignored in those early years and never subsequently made good. The school libraries that had been built up over many years in the grammar schools provided, in many cases, a solid foundation on which to build a larger and more varied collection, but this chance was not always taken and in the inevitable upheaval of total school and staff reorganisation the initiative was often lost.

Concurrent with the development of the comprehensive system for senior pupils, many areas decided also to restructure their educational provision for the younger age groups. Middle schools were set up to provide a bridge between the junior and senior pupils, and most authorities who decided on this pattern of schools opted for a system consisting of primary schools up to the age of nine, followed by a middle school for the next four years, then on to the comprehensive for the final years.

As with the introduction of comprehensive education, this involved a huge reallocation of existing resources as well as the need to provide for a different curriculum aimed at a new age group. Schools changed overnight from junior to middle or from senior to middle and staff changes in the early stages were very frequent as many found themselves to be square pegs in round holes. In the same way, many of a school's existing resources were quite unsuitable for the new intake, but with so many other initial problems to be solved, the library was low on the list. Some purpose-built middle schools opted for year group resource provision which sounded fine in theory but created problems in both administration and ongoing support.

Sixth-form colleges have been a further variation which some LEAs have adopted. Some parts of the country have had these for many years but others are now looking at the idea in more detail as falling rolls in senior schools create problems for the curriculum at the older age levels. Sixth-form colleges have done reasonably well (and in many cases much better than sixth-forms in schools) for library and resource provision and usually have a qualified librarian in charge and some ongoing financial support.

Present situation

A combination of stringent financial cut-backs, falling rolls and a government that wishes for more direct control of education has resulted in a state of flux over many areas of the country. Middle schools have already disappeared from some authorities who previously had them and variations on sixth-form colleges or a combined further education/post 16 + structure are in active consideration in many places. What this will do for libraries is anyone's guess but, in general, colleges have always done much better than schools, not only for libraries but also for librarians, so it may be that for the older pupil at least better times may be coming.

Special needs

This area falls half way between structural change and curriculum development and has implications for both. As a result largely of the Warnock Report, many children who had previously been educated in special schools, whether for reasons of physical handicap or learning difficulties, are now in the normal state schools and many special schools have in fact been closed. Current educational thinking and practice are very much towards mainstreaming and away from the more specialised, and some would argue isolating, special school provision. Although comparatively few children are involved, this has had an effect on the structure of schools and on the individual teachers in mainstream schools who have had to learn how to deal with children who may have special physical or behavioural needs and may need special teaching techniques to enable them to learn.

The resource implications will, of course, vary greatly depending not only on the type of handicap but also its level. Many children will be well able to use exactly the same resources as their peers, but other resources required may vary from large print books for a child of normal intelligence but partial sight to a collection of easy reading material for those with specific learning problems. What is not in doubt is that a relatively substantial amount of money will have to be spent to ensure that children with special needs are not expected to make do with unsuitable materials or second best. There may also be a need, in some instances, to provide special hardware in the library to help children with physical problems to use the resources.

CURRICULUM DEVELOPMENTS

The changes in the structure of schools, not the least being the grouping of all children into a comprehensive school rather than dividing them by ability at eleven, forced many teachers and subject departments into a reassessment of both their teaching content and their teaching method. Mixed ability teaching, always accepted and coped with in primary schools, suddenly became imperative for high schools. Much of grammar school teaching had relied on 'chalk and talk' but this was no longer an option when a very wide range of ability was found in most classes. The emphasis had to be on a more individualised approach and the pace of learning had to be related at least to groups of pupils and sometimes to an individual. This obviously involved teachers in a considerable amount of preparation but it also meant that, whereas previously one textbook or worksheet had served for the whole class, now a whole range of different resources had to be provided. For a time little was available and teachers had to find their own material but gradually publishers produced books and resources to fill this gap and the school library found itself increasingly called upon to provide a range of material on the same topic but at differing degrees of difficulty. Just as subject teachers had had to familiarise themselves with new materials and methods for the classroom situation, so the school librarian had to deal with all the varieties of subjects, levels and age groups and try to provide the learning resources to cover for all eventualities. Not surprisingly, few of them managed to even paper over the cracks – most were chronically short of money and even more had little or no time to spare from their own teaching duties.

Increasingly over the years the emphasis has changed in education from the 'product' to the 'process', and the teacher or lecturer has taken on the role of 'facilitator' rather than deliverer of information. This major shift involves a much greater co-operation between the teacher, the producer of resources and the organiser of the resources. All involved in this process need to have a wide range of knowledge of not only what exists, but where to get it and how best to use it for the student's advantage. Gone are the days when one standard textbook was enough to get a whole class through an examination, although the present move to more extensive and structured testing may yet bring that situation back. Topic work, assignments, projects all became common parlance for both teachers and pupils, but they all had the implicit reliance on access to individual resources and individual study. This was by no means always possible, and it seemed that the reality of resource provision had not kept pace with the demand.

Particular areas of curriculum change that have had a special effect on the school library include the following.

Information and study skills

Although some schools have always seen the importance of this aspect of the curriculum, it is only in fairly recent years that more attention nationally has been given to it. Particular impetus was given by the publication in 1981 of a Schools Council Curriculum Bulletin and since then many more teachers have become aware of the need for specialist teaching in this area. School librarians with their vital expertise and experience are in the forefront of this move and must be positive promoters of a 'whole-school' policy.

Multi-ethnic needs

Increasingly, as Britain has become a much more ethnically mixed society, so education has had to respond to this sociological change. From a eurocentric approach, both teaching and its resources have had to move towards a less biased view of world history and geography in particular and to reflect more closely the concerns and interests of many of today's pupils. This has had repercussions for the resource world in general and school libraries in particular. Much discarding and withdrawal of material which might prove offensive has had to be carried out and whole new criteria established for the purchase of replacement books and resources. School librarians have had to come to grips quickly with this new challenge and to ensure that suitable material is provided for all pupils.

Bilingualism and mother-tongue teaching

This is related to the growth of multi-ethnic Britain and by implication the variety of languages spoken by many of today's pupils and their families. The Welsh have for long led the rest of Britain in placing great emphasis on their language and culture and in insisting that this always has a place in the school curriculum. It is only relatively recently that the same stress has been placed on Urdu, Punjabi, Greek, or the many other languages spoken by children in British schools, and it is now quite common in some areas to find active support and teaching going on in schools in mother-tongue languages. This obviously has implications for the library in the school as books will be needed to reinforce this and to provide a variety of reading materials for children in their own languages.

New examination syllabus

Over the years since comprehensivisation, examination demands have changed quite substantially for senior pupils. From a nationally or regionally agreed and marked syllabus there has been a move, particularly through Mode 3 CSE, to internally set and marked exams. The previous 'essay' type answer has now been joined by multiple choice, oral examination, project work and continuous assessment. Again, the shift to independent learning with the teacher as helper and guide can be seen very clearly in the type of work now demanded from the pupil, but it also calls for a greatly increased resource bank on which to draw and on the expertise of both pupil and teacher to use it to its fullest potential.

The advent of the new GCSE aims to combine the best of both the old GCE and CSE examinations into one structure suitable for all abilities, and to stress problem-solving and the application of knowledge learned rather than an ability just to recall facts. GCSE is based on new approaches to learning involving individual research, oral and practical activities, assignments and the solving of particular problems. It will be noted that an even greater call will be made on resources to support such a change in overall approach, but it seems that, as this is written, little money, expertise or even thought has been given by the DES or many individual LEAs into how this need may be translated into reality.

The Manpower Services Commission and their impact on schools

The main thrust of MSC initiative in education has been felt in the field of further education but a certain amount has filtered into high schools and has had a distinct effect on the curriculum. The Technical and Vocational Education Initiative (TVEI) was set up to provide a broad cross-curricular learning experience for students of all abilities and was largely funded by the MSC as a pilot project for some LEAs. The main aim was to foster skills rather than transmit content and to include a substantial element of information technology. Many of these courses were set up with little or no co-operation with the resource experts and sometimes with a limited perception on the part of the course organisers of the role of information specialists, particularly in the area of information retrieval. Once more school librarians have been called upon to provide increased resources to support a new curriculum initiative.

Open Learning, the Open College and Open Access

These developments all concentrate on the adult learner (or at least the 16 +) at the moment but it may be that, in the future, schools may also take advantage of some of the options now open to individual students. All these initiatives have as their main aim the opening up of educational opportunity to all, regardless of either geographical situation or previous educational attainments. Some schools may well become centres for the Open College, but possibly the greatest impact will be on the development of distance learning packages and materials, the use of new technology to overcome distance problems and the much wider range of options open to any student anywhere. Again resource provision and access to resources will be a major element in the success or otherwise of these schemes.

The Core Curriculum and testing and monitoring

It is still too early to predict with any degree of accuracy what might be the impact of these two government initiatives. What does seem likely is that targets will be set for maths, English and science with testing, probably nationally, at regular intervals starting at the age of seven. The curriculum content and percentage of time to be spent on each area has been announced but how individual schools may respond to this is still unclear. Certainly the greatly increased time to be given to science subjects may cause problems given the existing shortage of science teachers. The resource implications are still unclear, too. It may mean a return to a much more structured approach with standard texts used throughout and little room left for individual study or research. However, this would contradict the stated aims of the GCSE in which emphasis is placed on problem-solving and the application of knowledge rather than any rote learning. What is not in doubt is that school librarians will again be called on to respond to this new 'timetable' and to provide whatever resource support is necessary.

IMPACT OF THE NEW TECHNOLOGIES

The 1960s and 70s saw a great explosion of 'machinery' into schools. The old lantern slide was rapidly replaced by filmstrips, film loops, slides and sound tapes. Multi-media kits became common and a facility to use all these items of software and control the necessary hardware became an essential part of teacher training and classroom expertise.

Since then, the world of 'hi-tech' has moved on and now virtually all schools have not only colour TVs but the video recorder as well. Children as well as teachers now expect a professional and sophisticated approach to the programmes they see and some of the earlier more amateurish filmstrips would not now be able to compete for a pupil's attention with a modern school's TV programme.

This approach to teaching relies heavily on a substantial capital expenditure for the machinery needed (and in many schools this means a number of pieces of equipment), an annual outlay on maintenance and money to provide the blank video tapes or pre-recorded material. Unless a school is very lucky in its capitation, this inevitably means that there is less money for everything else, and in many cases it is the book stock of a school that will suffer.

The rise of interactive video and other similar sophisticated developments may place yet more strain on a school budget as teachers naturally will wish to take advantage of recent technological innovations. It is already clear that this particular idea has great potential for skills teaching and also for some special need children who may have physical problems in writing or communicating in more normal ways. Again, though, the financial implications are large and as school budgets are certainly not growing at the moment, then it must mean a lowering of expenditure in other areas.

However, this growth of multi-media in all schools has led, in many cases, to school libraries that are genuine resource centres, stocking everything from slides, tapes, books and illustrations to computer programs. This involves the librarian in more work but does mean that the pupils and teachers can integrate much more effectively all forms of information regardless of type.

Computers

The advent of computers in schools and the subsequent phenomenal growth in their use has had an enormous impact on teachers at all levels and in all subjects. From an initial base in high school maths departments, they are now to be found in most primary classrooms and used for such diverse applications as helping in the teaching of reading to

A level economics. For teachers not brought up in the electronic age, it has not always been easy to adapt to this new and powerful medium, and most LEAs have spent, in conjunction with the DES, considerable sums of money on in-service training to equip all teachers with the necessary skills. Some forms of individualised learning are now a realistic alternative and for pupils with particular needs the computer program can often provide the specific learning package that they need.

The resource implications for this explosion of computers in schools are two-fold. On the one hand, the school as a whole has to make financial provision for the purchase and upkeep of the hardware, and also of all the various 'add-ons' needed ranging from ordinary computer printers to sophisticated peripherals which link computers in separate schools together or allow a school to become part of an external network. In addition, there is then the purchase of the relevant software for teaching purposes, often bought by individual subject departments. And last, but perhaps more importantly, there is the impact of computers on the school library.

Computerised information retrieval has long been an accepted and understood part of professional librarianship and many librarians have had years of experience in this field. However, for many teachers, and by implication for some school librarians, this is a very new field and one still imperfectly understood. The school librarian's role is a crucial one here and if the initiative is not grasped, then many pupils are being denied a vital element in their education. School librarians, at all levels of education, need time and training to help them to introduce computers into their library and to train pupils in information retrieval techniques. Computer programs should become a normal part of the library stock but, again this has implications both in terms of the money available and time allowed for library organisation.

Together with computers, TVs and videos are also information sources and more and more schools are beginning to make use of services like Viewdata and Teletext. Again, the school librarian has to keep abreast of this rapidly developing field and make sure that all students can make use of these sources of information.

CONCLUSIONS

It would seem from this brief catalogue of educational change and development over the last few years that most are concerned with the high schools, or certainly the older pupil. In one sense this is true as the direct effect of such a major change as the introduction of the comprehensive school had an immediate impact on all pupils and teachers in that sector. Recent innovations such as GCSE, will also be felt initially by high school teachers but, although it may take time to percolate, all educational change is felt throughout the whole system and no one tier or type of school can work in isolation from another. The insistence on problem-solving techniques for GCSE will be reflected in teaching approaches throughout all age ranges, and such elements as a multi-ethnic syllabus or an acceptance of languages other than English often had their roots in curriculum development in the Primary school sector.

What is not in any doubt is that all these changes have had resource implications and that, for many schools and teachers, it has been impossible to reflect accurately these new approaches in the resources provided. Money has become progressively tighter both for staff and resources and, as so often is the case in libraries of all types, they are the first to suffer in any cut-back.

This chapter has attempted to show some of the recent moves in schools and to draw attention to what that means for the school library. Further chapters will look in more detail at school libraries and how they can best respond to new ideas and new innovations.

2
The Historical Development of the School Library

School libraries have always been expected to respond to change within the educational system even though the pace of this has been much quicker over the last few years. Some of the seeds of the present problems in school library provision and the role of school librarians can be traced back to earlier developments and help to explain the present situation and perhaps suggest solutions.

THE EARLY YEARS

The major public schools—and also very many of the long established grammar schools—had always maintained substantial school libraries mainly based on the tradition of Oxford and Cambridge colleges and their libraries. In these schools the libraries were seen as an important part of the educational process, but it was not until the early years of this century that this movement began to filter more widely into education generally. The then Board of Education began to take an interest in 1906 when it said that every new secondary school should have a school library, and in 1931 it published a pamphlet on secondary school building which included a special section on the library. Economically, though, this was a very bad time with unemployment rife and with the infamous Geddes axe falling on education, There was cetainly no money available for new initiatives.

However, at the same time as government was showing signs of interest, there was also a groundswell of enthusiasm from the teachers themselves who in many cases were beginning to build up a fund of experience and expertise in running school libraries. In 1935 the Board of Education held its first course for teacher-librarians so reflecting the increasing interest in this area, and in 1936 the Carnegie United Kingdom Trust was persuaded to hold an enquiry into the prevailing situation which showed, on the whole, a most unsatisfactory state of affairs. This led to the founding in 1937 of the School Library Association, and also to the Library Association starting a group for school librarians (although this latter had only a short life). In 1937 also came the first publication of *The School Librarian*, the journal of the SLA. In these early stages, relationships between the SLA and the Library Association were often strained, partly because of the differing perceptions of the role of the school librarian and the qualifications needed to fulfil this role. (It should be noted that some of that wariness still lingers on today.)

POSTWAR DEVELOPMENTS

The Second World War effectively stopped any further expansion and it was not until 1945 that the movement towards better school libraries began to press forward again. In 1945 came the publication of a joint report by the SLA and LA calling for increases in the training of student teachers in the area of resource management, and in the 1950s the LA called for a policy of professional librarians in all schools which, of course, had very direct implications for many members of the SLA who were teacher-librarians. This action was seen as rather a threat by the SLA, but, in fact, good did come of it as the two bodies joined together to establish the Joint Certificate in School Library Studies which was aimed at giving teachers an understanding of and grounding in basic library skills and was validated by both bodies.

As the movement towards the greater provision of school libraries gained momentum, so it became increasingly obvious that some nationally agreed standards were necessary. The Library Association published their first Standards in 1970, and although they were fairly careful over questions of staffing, they did suggest that all schools with over 800 pupils should have a chartered librarian. Most schools had at that time teacher-librarians who were trying to combine the duties of a class teacher with the organisation and day-to-day running of the school library. (Today, this has not altered very much in vast areas of the country!) However, some LEAs, notably the Inner London Education Authority (ILEA), were beginning to move towards a policy of employing chartered librarians in some of their larger schools. This trend has certainly increased over the last few years, although the harsh economic climate of the 1970s and 1980s has meant little expansion in any field of education. The SLA has continued to support the cause of teacher-librarians and to do all it can to help by means of publications, courses and meetings.

THE SCHOOL LIBRARY IN THE 1980s

After the initial publication of the LA Standards in 1970, there has been a growth in publications, either by official bodies or interested groups, about school libraries and librarianship. Noteworthy by its absence, however, has been any official government statement backed by any legislation or even any national guidelines with Department of Education and Science or Office of Arts and Libraries backing. In 1973, the LA issued an update of its Standards incorporating a statement on non-book materials. This reflected the increased use in schools of multimedia and of the need for the school librarian to be aware of this demand and to respond to it. In 1977, the LA produced a completely new set of guidelines which took into account the recent trends in education, notably the move to comprehensive schools, and also the increased emphasis on independent learning and new teaching methods, with all that implied for resource provision and organisation. In *Libraries in Secondary Schools,* issued by the SLA in 1972, the emphasis was more on the educational role of the library and objectives of the librarian in that context rather than any 'library skills' approach. *The Way Ahead* published in 1980 was a major policy statement by the SLA on its overall philosophy and future intent. Unfortunately, its publication coincided with the beginning of the present very harsh economic climate, and although the SLA made great efforts both to promote and publicise this, the overall emphasis on cuts and containment were not conducive to any real consideration of an appraisal of roles, never mind any proposed expansion of services.

There were some stirrings, though, at national level and the result of these did at last provide some facts and figures to the hitherto often expressed but never proven criticism of school library provision. In 1981, the DES published its Statistical Bulletin 7/81, the result of a 10% survey into library provision in all maintained secondary schools in England. It threw up a horrifying picture of neglect reinforcing all that had been said for many years by people working in the field. The DES followed this in 1985 with a survey of secondary school libraries in six local authorities. Again, it proved that the problems had not gone away and that nothing had radically changed. These two reports from the Inspectorate of the DES proved to be most useful ammunition for those fighting for better school libraries.

What may yet prove to be one of the most important documents produced on school libraries was published in 1984. *School Libraries: The Foundations of the Curriculum* was the result of a committee set up by the Library and Information Services Committee to look into the whole question of the future of school library provision. LISC is an advisory body to the Office of Arts and Libraries on various matters to do with library provision, but this was the first time that attention had been paid by it to the question of libraries in schools. Their report could only be a recommendation and it had no legislative teeth, but it was the first to be published by a government department and has had, and continues to have, much influence on LEAs as well as with all the professional bodies involved in school librarianship. Its main recommendations, all very clearly and concisely set out, argue that the school library has an essential and central task in the school curriculum. The library should be the hub around which all learning takes place and should be the motivating force in the planning and implementation of a study and information skills curriculum. The report provides a list of recommended steps applicable to the various people involved in school library provision from, on the one hand, the teacher-librarian, to the LEA at the other end of the scale. It is required reading for anyone concerned with resource provision in schools at whatever level.

Another important source of information on school libraries, albeit taking more time and trouble to unearth, is the collection of facts and figures to be found in the HMI reports on individual schools. Work has been done to try and pull some of this together but as the DES appears not to lay down guidelines for its Inspectors for checking on library provision in schools, the resulting information is bound to be patchy. As yet no qualified librarians are employed by the DES so this area of school's resources (and its great potential for curriculum support) is only ever checked by an 'amateur'— even if an enthusiastic one.

The publication of the LISC report and the subsequent publicity generated by it has sparked many authorities to attempt to produce some local guidelines and standards for their own areas. In 1982, Northamptonshire Education Committee produced its *Library Provision in Secon-*

dary Education document and Devon published *Secondary School Libraries* in 1985. Avon in their *Guidelines for the Provision of Library Resources* included all age-ranges and in many authorities similiar initiatives are being taken. Berkshire is at present mounting a research project to clarify the objectives of the school library and to design a pro-gramme for policy implementation. In 1985, the Scottish equivalent of the earlier English LISC report was published and this also showed very clearly the swing towards curriculum-related thinking for school libraries and the need for suitably qualified staff to implement this.

It would seem from all the evidence that this move towards a more professional and curriculum-based library will continue, and given many of the present education initiatives, for instance GCSE, then the pressure for a better school library service will not disappear.

3
The Present Situation

CURRENT PROVISION OF SCHOOL LIBRARIES AND LIBRARIANS

The present situation in the provision of school libraries and librarians in the UK is one of great disparity both in terms of structural organisation and in resource provision. Some areas of the country have a policy of employing chartered librarians in all high schools and even provide some professional support in primary schools; other areas rely on teacher-librarians to provide whatever is possible. Some LEAs have carefully thought-out objectives for their school libraries and have rolling programmes to implement these, but many education authorities have absolutely no policy at all and it is left very much to an individual school, its head and teacher-librarian to decide the library policy. The recent economic gloom has only served to make the position worse and even in some of those authorities with a good record, services and resources have had to be reduced. Cuts in staffing in schools have resulted in many teacher-librarians having even less time to spend on library organisation, and as there have never been any statutory rules or even guidelines about time for the library, many teachers find themselves with virtually no free periods for this activity. In many LEAs expansion of chartered librarians into schools has had to be delayed and plans shelved.

A depressing picture was painted by the HMI report published in 1986. It stated: 'There was a decrease in the number of chartered librarians in schools and the situation of school libraries was assessed as satisfactory in only 18 authorities and less than satisfactory or poor in no less that 73 LEAs. Many libraries are under-developed, under-used and their availabilty to pupils often restricted.' Press reports frequently tell of parents supporting not only the school library with money and donations but even paying for classroom texts as well. Although some areas have managed to maintain their school libraries to a reasonable standard, it is again the case, as so often in education, that where you live is all-important in terms of the educational services you receive.

It seems pertinent to ask why school libraries are in such a state of disarray and chaos and no national policy is even available never mind widely applied. Considerably more fuss is made by both teachers and parents if dinner-ladies are threatened than if a school's resources are about to be cut. There would seem to be two main reasons why this should be the case. First there is a lack of any soundly based research on which to prove the case for school libraries, and which both links and reinforces their role in the context of the educational objectives of the school. The second reason is the long-running discussion (not to say on some occasions argument) about whether teachers or librarians should run school libraries. This latter question has often resulted in allowing both the DES and uninterested local LEAs to ignore the whole question of provision and rely on a policy of 'divide and rule'. The research lack is slowly being remedied but the body of evidence is still small and a complete picture is only slowly emerging. Certainly, recent HMI reports have shown up the disastrous state of many school libraries, and ones such as the Statistical Bulletin 7/81 and the *Survey of Secondary School Library Provision in Six Local Authorities* have added much to the jig-saw. The overall impression in this later survey was that 'many libraries were inadequately staffed and stocked, poorly financed and under-used.'

Coupled with the increasing evidence from the HMI reports into individual schools, a nationwide picture of provision is becoming clearer. This at least provides a base from which to move and many education authorities and school library services have initiated their own surveys into provision for their own areas. Without this information foundation, it is impossible to mount any relevant research but much more work is now being undertaken and the whole field of school librarianship and its links with the curriculum and learning are coming under much more scrutiny. Previously, the case for a school library rested on the premise that a library is a 'good thing', and until recently any attempt to justify that in an objective and proven way would have been very difficult for even the most enthusiastic and informed professional. For far too long have many school libraries been seen either as prestige places for governors' meetings or, alternatively, 'sin-bins' for the recalcitrant. Until the role of the library can be accepted and understood by all in education (and particularly those who make and enforce policy) then school libraries, for much of the country at least, are unlikely to progress at all. One of the repercussions of this vacuum is that many LEAs feel under no compulsion even to think about a policy for school libraries never mind actually implement one. Those authorities which do have a policy are probably those which are more innovative and forward-looking, and also the ones which already have a strong and influential school library service to make the case for the development of professional service in schools. It seems an odd state of affairs that school librarianship has been so slow to provide itself with a carefully thought-out and argued rationale. Unlike many other areas of librarianship it does have a clearly defined 'community' and an agreed set of objectives. It should not be too difficult for the role of the school library to be linked into this.

Although it is not necessarily the case that all 'good' education authorities will have professional librarians in schools, certainly very many of them do, and this has serious implications for the future staffing of school libraries nationwide. Those who make and monitor national education policy may well perceive the best school libraries to be run by professional librarians and so be influenced to encourage this move. This is not altogether a fair assumption as most school librarians will probably have no other responsibilities and will be able to give all their time and attention to the running of the library. They will obviously bring all the organisational skills of librarianship to the task and so be able to present a well-run and effective service. The teacher-librarian, by contrast, will probably have nearly a full teaching timetable and be faced with running the library in breaks, dinner-hours and much of their own time. Neither will most of them have had the benefit of any sustained training in the skills of librarianship and so will find the day-to-day tasks more difficult and more time-consuming. In the DES Statistical Bulletin 7/81 69% of teachers in charge of school libraries had had no special training and were allowed an average of 4½ hours per week for their library responsibilities! However, where their great strength lies is in their knowledge and experience in education and in teaching methods, an expertise that is lacking in most librarians. This understanding is really a vital component for the good school library so any measurement that does not take account of the very different responsibilities and duties of librarians as opposed to teacher-librarians cannot give a realistic picture, nor should it be used to justify the case for more professional library staff as opposed to teacher-librarians. It has yet to be proved how effective a school library could be if run by a teacher who has basic library skills under the same time provision as a librarian.

RESPONSIBILITY FOR THE LIBRARY

In high schools, it is very rare to find a teacher-librarian who is not part of the English department, and this also has led in some instances to a weakening of the case for school libraries. This traditional role for the English teacher seems to be based on the theory that English equals reading equals books equals libraries, and presupposes that other departments have neither the need nor the capability either to read books or run a library. This is quite obviously a nonsense but it is very rarely questioned by either teachers or education management and is reinforced by the local English advisor often being given responsibility for overseeing school libraries, although the chances are that they will know no more about library operation than the poor teacher-librarian—and quite possibly less. The DES are equally guilty as they appoint to their Inspectorate an English specialist to look after school libraries in addition to their normal English responsibilities.

There may have been a case to be made for this when the grammar schools were beginning to think seriously about libraries and the education offered had a considerably more 'classical' bent than it has in the comprehensive system. Now, it seems to make little or no sense to continue this staffing structure as the norm for all teacher-librarians, but as hierarchies and departmental structures have been built over many years with this expectation, it is not easy to break. However, with the emergence of information technology and information skills, it becomes imperative that the librarian of a school has not only the knowledge but also the experience and expertise to bring to this very important area of the curriculum. Whilst some English teachers may well be interested and aware, it is quite probable that there will be teachers in other departments who may be better able to encourage and promote this aspect through the school library. It could be argued that a scientist's training with an emphasis on logical thinking and procedures would be better able to bring not only the ability to cope with the organisational skills so necessary for the running of any library, but also considerable experience in computerisation and technology. The selection of resources can also suffer at the hands of any relatively inexperienced teacher and this long tradition of always having an English teacher in charge can sometimes be seen in the rather 'literary' content of the stock, to the possible detriment of other subject areas. What is important is to have an enthusiastic, knowledgeable and 'crusading' person in charge of the school library with sufficient status in the school to influence management decisions. Which teaching department supplies that teacher should not be predetermined but based on who within the school is most able and willing to provide a good service.

A most important factor in the present low status of school libraries and, by implication, school librarians is that the vast majority are a long way down the school's hierarchy and have little or no influence over school policy. It is unusual to find a teacher-librarian very far up the ladder and very many of them are still near the bottom in terms of either promotion prospects or departmental responsibilities. This gives them no real voice or influence and so, again, the role of the school library is seen as peripheral to much of the life and work of the school. Even where professional librarians are employed, their status is not necessarily any better and they, also, may be denied access to curriculum committees, heads of department meetings and similiar decision-making bodies. It is true, though, that professional librarians may be in a better position to argue the case for resources as they usually have not only the powerful voice of the School Library Service behind them, but in many cases, they are actually employed by this service and so are not so dependant on perhaps a head of department's goodwill or so beset by conflicting loyalties. They also have the great advantage of objectivity and should be able to speak directly to the top management in the school.

THE WAY FORWARD: DUAL QUALIFICATIONS?

Is there any way through this wilderness of patchy provision, differing staffing structures and, in many schools, a library that resembles a jumble-sale collection and makes any idea of links with the curriculum a mere joke?

For many years it has been the official policy of both the Library Association and the School Library Association to support the principle of dual qualifications for all school librarians. There is little doubt that this would be of great benefit to the individuals concerned and also provide their institutions with the potential for a school library and resource centre which really could be at the heart of all learning. The marrying together of educational and librarianship principles certainly seems the logical and obvious step needed, and for many countries overseas, notably the USA, Canada and Australia, this is no myth but an accepted and much approved reality for all who wish to work in the field of school librarianship. This insistence on a dual qualification (first as a teacher then followed by study in librarianship) has played a distinct part in raising not only the standard of service given and expected in schools in these countries, but also in the standing and prestige of school librarians and school libraries.

However, for most teachers and virtually all librarians in the United Kingdom, the reality of obtaining a dual qualification is a myth. As Norman Beswick so rightly remarked, neither the DES nor any of the other official bodies involved give either reward, increased status or even official recognition for such qualifications so it is not surprising that individuals are reluctant to embark on such a demanding course of study. If you can get a job with only one professional qualification at the same salary and status (both probably very low) as you would get if you had two, there is little incentive to widen your skills.

FURTHER QUALIFICATIONS FOR TEACHERS

For the persistent teacher who wishes to qualify as a librarian as well there are some avenues open, but it is much more restricted for the librarian wishing to become a teacher. There has always been a commitment to in-service training for teachers and a budget to provide this. The need for an updating of old skills and the learning of new ones is an important part of most LEAs provision and this will vary from short courses run at the local teachers' centre to year-long secondments for higher qualifications or research. This facility may allow teachers wishing to obtain a qualification in librarianship to be seconded to a postgraduate course in librarianship. With the coming of the all-graduate teaching profession, entry to these courses is now becoming much easier for teachers but it still presupposes a supportive LEA and, in many instances, the geographical nearness of a suitable course.

The emergence of Masters degrees and other similiar high level courses in librarianship has meant that teachers may be able to gain admittance to these also, but, not surprisingly, many are more than reluctant to return to the previous low status and low salary of school librarianship when their increased skills may well open other doors. This type of course, interesting and challenging though it may be for the student, makes no pretence to train people in basic library skills so it may well leave the teacher-librarian no better equipped to cope with the day-to-day library operations. It also has to be remembered that not all these higher-level courses are recognised by the Library Association for inclusion on their professional register so openings in other areas of librarianship could remain closed.

For the very many teachers who do not want to embark on a second qualification but are faced with the task of running a school library, the outlook for any lower level training is bleak. Until 1986, the Library Association and the School Library Association co-operated to validate jointly a Certificate in School Library Studies. This gave very many teachers throughout the UK an opportunity to pursue a relevant course, one in which the syllabus allowed for the student's direct experience and needs to be taken into account and also allowed for a substantial amount of assessed work. It was a carefully thought-out scheme and allowed for individual colleges throughout the country to mount their own local courses after validation by the parent body. Unfortunately, it gradually failed to attract enough potential students, probably for two main reasons. It was a two-year part-time course which demanded much in terms of student time and effort but, as with the dual qualification argument, led to no official recognition on successful completion of the course.

At the same time as this course was on offer, many teachers were taking OU degrees, part-time BEds and a host of other qualifications most of which demanded a similiar amount of effort but which had tangible rewards in terms of salary or promotion prospects. Coupled with these two very obvious drawbacks, the latter years of the Certificate saw the beginning of the harsh cuts in the education budget and both staffing and resources came under increasing pressure. Many teachers felt unwilling to commit themselves to a two-year course of study in the climate prevailing in the late 1970s and 80s. In view of all these factors, it was little wonder that teacher-librarians decided that they could more usefully employ their time on other things!

A variation on the two-year official course emerged in various parts of the country when an individual college would decide to shorten the course to only one year and issue their own college or polytechnic certificate. These, of course, had no national standing but, locally, proved to be a much more popular option.

Eventually the decision was reached to discontinue the LA and SLA qualification, and currently there is no recognised national route by which any teacher can obtain some basic librarianship skills, although initiatives by individual colleges do provide the opportunity for study in some areas of the country. Validation for these courses is provided by a bewildering array of bodies, ranging from Leicester University for the course run at Nene College in Northamptonshire to the CNAA for the course at Bristol Polytechnic. Virtually all these courses are provided by institutions which have had a long history of running the Certificate course and are in well populated areas with a pool of potential recruits.

For the teacher away from such a centre, there is nothing on offer at all unless their own LEA in-service programme provides some support. It maybe that if the School Library Service is an influential voice in a particular area, courses run by them for local teachers may be available, but however good these are, they cannot provide the comprehensive input that a recognised course of study will involve. They may also take account of local variations and conditions and so may not equip the teacher-librarian with skills that are readily transferable.

The only hope, on any national basis, would seem to lie with distance learning packages. These have already been developed for a City and Guilds examination for Library Assistants and allow students from all geographical locations to study and learn for a recognised qualification. However, this type of learning has two major implications—first that there is a validating body prepared to oversee the syllabus and examinations, and secondly that there is both the money and the expertise available to develop the actual packages and provide the administrative and professional back-up necessary. There is little sign at the moment of either of these two prerequisites and the situation for many teacher-librarians is increasingly dire.

For the foreseeable future, and certainly well into the next century, the teachers themselves in most high schools and all primary schools are going to be faced with running their school libraries. How well they do that will depend in large measure on the training and support they receive. Many of them at the moment receive little of either.

FURTHER QUALIFICATIONS FOR LIBRARIANS

If anything, librarians have an even tougher time than teachers in their pursuit of a futher qualification. There has never been the commitment to an in-service programme or budget as obtains in the educational world and it is very rare to hear of a librarian being seconded to a course of even part-time study.

The barriers to a school librarian becoming a qualified teacher are formidable and it is much easier to start off as a teacher and then become a librarian than the other way round! One of the problems for the would-be teacher is the insistence on teaching practice and the probationary year of work before final qualification. This in itself precludes many librarians from pursuing the course, although as librarianship has been an all-graduate profession for many years, librarians would be qualified for a place on a PGCE course.

For some lucky librarians working in the further education sector, it has been easier to qualify as a teacher through the initiative of the DES in encouraging many of the craft and technical staff in colleges, many of whom had no prior teaching qualification or experience, to attend part-time courses leading to full teaching status. This method allowed for a number of tutor-librarians to become dually qualified but this still left the vast majority in schools with no real hope of finding a suitable course.

Many of the school library services throughout the country mount extensive in-service programmes for their school librarians to help them gain expertise in the fields of education and teaching method, and whilst obviously this can only add to the librarian's understanding and skill level, it is still no real substitute for a sustained period of study and the associated practice.

The future looks bleak for any-one interested in becoming dually qualified and hardly any better for those just wanting a little 'first-aid' in an unfamiliar skill. Those who run school libraries, whether as teachers or librarians, are only a very small and insignificant part of the total LEA staff and their call for both courses and the money to run them will come well down the list of priorities. Pressure to cut costs, close undersubscribed courses and halt any expansion, all mean that school librarians are very unlikely to find anything new on offer and the chances are that even what has existed in the past may well be closed down. Since the Library Association and the School Library Association ceased to be involved there is now no central record of courses which do exist so even the most enthusiastic teacher or librarian is going to have problems in even finding out what courses are running. School librarianship in Great Britian has suffered throughout its history over the lack of a nationally qualified and recognised workforce together with the status that being so qualified would give. This situation shows no signs of improving.

An additional problem that now affects the professional education of librarians is a change in the emphasis of the syllabus followed by most institutions. For many years, courses offered students the opportunity, as one element in their course, to specialise in a particular area of librarianship. Schools and children's work was usually one of the options so many students graduated from library school with some special understanding and knowledge of this area of work. However, in recent years most of these options have been dropped and librarianship education is increasingly seen as being of a 'generalist' nature so, in theory at least, equipping the new entrant to the profession to take up any post anywhere.

There would seem to be two factors at work here and one is undoubtedly the financial and economic argument. It takes valuable staff time and relevant expertise to mount these various options and most institutions are under constant pressure to cut costs. Cutting out this additional expenditure is one easy way. Additionally, more and more stress is being placed on the information technology aspect of librarianship. Although this is undoubtedly a very important aspect of the future in librarianship, it seems to many commentators that the right balance has not been struck. Too much emphasis on 'machines' and not enough on the information needs of the people they should serve can only be detrimental to the profession as a whole. The end effect of this for schools is that, whereas in the past many school librarians came into the work with some prior training and knowledge, now it is unusual to find a young librarian who has covered any aspect of children's work in his or her degree.

CONCLUSIONS

The overall worsening of the situation for all school librarians, whether teachers or professional librarians, coincided with the release of probably the most important document on school libraries to be published. *School Libraries: The Foundations of the Curriculum* was the result of a committee set up by the Library and Information Services Council (LISC) to look into the provision of school library services and how best they could meet children's educational needs. It is a document that details in explicit and easily understood steps how librarians, teachers, heads, LEAs, the DES and all the other bodies involved can implement a policy to ensure that the school library becomes a real force within the school and a vital element in all learning. In many education authorities with a good record of school library provision, this report has been the focus of not only much discussion but also action to put into practice many of its recommendations. Unfortunately, it has fallen like a stone in many parts of the country where school libraries are not seen as important or integral to any real learning, and so the disparity grows between different parts of the country. All this at a time when the new GCSE places so much emphasis on individual research and problem-solving!

It seems unlikely that in the present era of 'accountability' which seems to pervade all official thinking that the situation either in individual schools or for individual school librarians will improve. There seems little evidence of any new courses or training schemes for teacher librarians—they will be left to battle on as best they can with, in most cases, very little support either from within their school or externally. The numbers of professional librarians will probably not increase very much at all and the outlook seems bleak.

4
The Role of the Library in the Curriculum

The recent report *School Libraries: the Foundations of the Curriculum* is a reinforcement and restatement of all that many school librarians have felt and tried to practise over very many years. Libraries of all types have seen themselves as being in the forefront of educational aspiration and in particular of self-help and independent study. The original public libraries set up in the latter half of the nineteenth century were very much the children of the old Mechanics Institutes and their function was closely tied to the whole concept of self-help and independent learning. Only relatively recently have they been seen also as a source of much recreational material. In the same way school libraries have always been very much a part of the educational process but it is perhaps only recently that the emphasis has changed from that of offering a relatively passive resource and study facility to that of a positive initiative in promoting not only the better use of what may be available and encouraging different learning strategies in handling these resources, but also in leading moves that prepare pupils to handle information better whether in conventional printed form or increasingly, via a computer or other technical means.

THE ROLE OF THE LIBRARY

Since the early days of libraries there has been not only an explosion of knowledge (and, by implication, of new subjects as well) but also a change in the whole nature of information and of the skills needed to use it to the full. The volume of publishing has increased enormously to keep up with this expansion in knowledge, and the skills needed to access it have also increased in complexity. The way in which this knowledge is used has also changed, and this in turn puts greater demands on both the librarian and the library's users.

In 1978 Arthur Little, an American, defined three eras of knowledge.

He postulated that knowledge for knowledge's sake was the most important factor pre-1940. Then followed a period of what he called 'mission orientated' knowledge, i.e. the information needed to do a particular job. Now he feels that the emphasis is on using knowledge in problem-solving situations, so not only do we now need access to a much greater bank of information, but we also need much greater skills to track down what is relevant and then subsequently evaluate what we find.

It is interesting to note that when one looks at the new GCSE examination all the pointers suggest that Little was right in his analysis of future information needs and use. If school libraries are to fulfil their central role in the school curriculum then much rethinking will be needed. On present evidence it would appear that most school libraries have hardly reached stage two of Little's hypothesis and will have far to go not only in the provision of actual resources but also in facing the much harder task of attitude and role perception affecting both the school librarian and the view of them held by their teaching colleagues.

What is becoming increasingly clear is that all libraries, including those in schools, have to be able to justify their roles and their relevance to their 'clients'. The accent is now on accountability and the monitoring of public services, and education has been one of the targets for this exercise. School libraries must be seen to be an intrinsic and invaluable element in the learning process and to be able to prove that they are a 'cost-effective' part of the total school resources. For school libraries this means having a clearly defined part to play in the whole teaching and learning programme for all pupils and being inextricably tied to the objectives and philosophy of the school.

From what little evidence does exist it would seem that the most successful school libraries are those that are in the vanguard of curriculum support, and these should supply their less fortunate colleagues with role models that they could copy. Only by being integrated into the total learning objectives and philosophy of the school can the school library hope not only to survive but also to grow in independence and importance. The school library has to be aware, as all in education must, of the expectations of the world outside the school door, as well as the demands of examinations and differing curricula inside the school, and so ensure that the skills that society demands from its adults are incorporated into everyday school life. This will increasingly mean the ability to handle information that may be in a variety of formats and to be competent and confident in handling the whole field of information technology. Libraries of all types have traditionally provided a 'window onto the world' and school libraries must maintain this outward philosophy.

How, then, does the school librarian, whether teacher or professional librarian, set about the task of ensuring that the library is not only relevant to the needs of all its potential customers but is also playing a positive and enthusiastic role in the whole learning process? Recently more and more helpful and positive ideas have surfaced, many in the wake of the LISC document. This latter, though, is the most influential and far-reaching of all the relevant publications and it should always be the starting point for anyone wishing to involve their school library much more heavily into the total learning experience. This report notes some of the reasons why school libraries have failed to make any real impact, amongst which are the following:

1. Isolation of librarians from curriculum planning.
2. Too much emphasis on resource provision to the exclusion of resource use.
3. No 'whole-school' planning or strategy for learning.
4. Lack of a generally accepted policy for the library and librarian.
5. Low status and role perception of both the librarian and the library on the part of the rest of the staff.
6. Often inadequate staffing in terms of both expertise and time available.
7. Insufficient funding.
8. Accommodation and space problems.
9. Stock that is often old, dirty and irrelevant to most pupils' needs.

It would seem from this catalogue of woe – and few school libraries will not admit to at least some of these problems – that there is much work to be done, particularly in the area of public relations, before the school library can be the powerhouse that it should be.

THE LIBRARY POLICY DOCUMENT

It would seem that the essential start to this process is the formulation of a policy document for the library. This will not only provide all involved in the exercise with an opportunity to analyse the existing situation but also enable them to look ahead and plan for future development. The formulation of a well-thought out policy for any task is important for the following reasons:

1. It helps in the definition of aims and objectives.
2. It encourages the formulation of strategies to carry out the objectives.
3. It analyses the resource provision and resource needs.
4. It addresses the question of role definition and of position within the hierarchy.
5. It incorporates evaluation procedures.

Benefits which accrue from having such a policy document would include the greater understanding on the part of the rest of the staff of the library's role, a better 'match' between user and resources, closer integration of the librarian into the teaching, and a greater influence on both financial and management decisions affecting the library. Questions which help to clarify the priorities for a policy include:

1. Why are we doing this?
2. What do we hope to achieve?
3. Who benefits?
4. What is the cost in both staffing and financial terms?
5. Are we doing it efficiently?
6. Is it effective?
7. Could it be achieved by any better means?
8. Can we become more effective and at what cost?
9. What happens if we do nothing?
10. How do we know if we are succeeding?

As individual schools differ, so will their own particular library policies. There is no carbon copy that all schools could, or should, adopt. However, it is likely that all schools may well have some or all of the following:

1. An overall strategy for linking the library to the overall teaching in the school which would be discussed and decided at top manage-

ment level. The head and department heads would be represented on this committee as well as the school librarian. They would formulate the statement of intent from which all further, perhaps more detailed, policies would follow

2. A whole-school policy for a library, study and information skills course headed by the school librarian (acting as head of department for this). This would be worked out by staff from all the relevant departments but would have the backing and authority incorporated in the main policy statement.
3. A policy for the library and its staff to ensure that all the aims and objectives of the main statement could be met. This would probably be decided by a group which included the library staff but also representives of other departments.
4. An internal 'library' policy for all the library staff dealing with the day-to-day management and organisation and ensuring that all the policy decisions are incorporated into the necessary library routines.
5. A policy for the evaluation and monitoring of the library and of the study skills curriculum, and for the development and future extension of library involvement.

To make your own decisions on what to include in the policy document, or exclude from it, you will need to take the following into consideration:

1. The age-range of the pupils.
2. The general philosophy and objectives of the school. (If you are very lucky these may have been written down!)
3. The curriculum and, most importantly, teaching methods which may vary considerably from year group to year group or with ability levels.
4. Present resource provision within the school and what exists externally.
5. The internal management structure of the school and an understanding of how decisions are made.
6. An understanding of national trends in education and the effect they may have on your school.
7. A willingness to change and to look for positive benefits in new ideas.

The lack of a library policy which is understood by all staff and has the backing of the head and all the top school management creates a vacuum. In the vast majority of cases this vacuum will be filled by a very negative view of the library, and in all major decisions its presence and that of its staff will be ignored. If you, as the school librarian, do not press for a policy then certainly no one else will. The repercussions of this are enormous and can be seen in many schools today. Lack of resources for the library because it is not considered important enough, staff with little support from their colleagues and even less time allocation, all create a vicious circle of deprivation and neglect which serves to push the library even further away from any real role or purpose. If you have no idea where you are going, how do you know when you have arrived? Time spent with colleagues on evolving a policy for the library can never be time wasted and all school librarians should put it to the very top of their priority list. Amongst the benefits of this are the following:

1. The library – and the librarian – are seen as being an integral part of the school and of the whole learning process.
2. Perceptions of the rest of the staff about the library and its role are influenced and gradually changed.
3. The library's profile is more evident and so any call for higher spending or more resources has more chance of success.
4. User needs can be readily identified and strategies evolved to meet these.
5. An agreed and implemented plan for a study skills curriculum involves the library in all areas of the school and with all the pupils. It ensures a central role for the library and the incorporation of it into all subject departments.
6. Last, but by no means least, a library policy properly planned and implemented will ensure that all pupils have access to teaching in the whole field of information management and retrieval, both through conventional print methods and computerised processes.

It makes little difference what type of school you are in as a policy is still vital in any situation, although the policy for a primary school may obviously be less detailed than that for a high school. In a book of case studies of successful school libraries, Margaret Marshall McDonald attempted to analyse the ingredients necessary to ensure that the library was an integal and important part of the school. Central to this was the whole-hearted support and commitment of the head and the rest of the 'top management'. This ensured not only the right climate of opinion in which to work but in a practical sense safeguarded the provision of the vital resources, both human and financial. The second reason for success was the implementation of a whole-school policy for a library and study skills curriculum, but without the initial backing of the head this latter would have been difficult to achieve. The librarians, with their own enthusiasm, expertise and knowledge, were vital to the success of the school library.

PROMOTING THE LIBRARY

As well as making steps towards library policy, a study skills curriculum, etc, there are also other ways the school librarian can use to generate interest and excitement. Amongst these would be the following:

1. Show a high profile to the rest of the staff. Many school librarians suffer from the 'dogsbody' syndrome when their own perception of their role is that of a downtrodden, harassed and undervalued member of staff. Inevitably, this view will be passed on to other members of staff, so not only does the individual suffer from this lack of perceived status, so does the library. This syndrome is possibly more common in schools where there has been a tradition of teacher-librarians (probably short on time, money and expertise) but it can still affect professional librarians, particularly if they are the first professional to run the library after many years of a hard-pressed teacher trying to cope.

2. Try all the marketing techniques possible! Encourage displays around the school, link up with projects that are being undertaken in subject departments and get all the help possible from other agencies like the School Library Service, School Museums Service or anything else available in the area. Encourage staff to make suggestions and feel involved themselves in the library, and if in the process of all this, you create more demand than you can fulfil, then you should have a cast-iron case for more money, more time and more resources.

3. Look critically at how the library sells itself to the school. What image does it project? Imagine you are a visitor to the school and there is no one to question. What could you tell about the library and its effect on the school? Is the library a victim of old notices and dusty book-jackets pinned up ages ago and forgotten? Are current periodicals mixed up with the back copies, and where is the current copy of *The Times Educational Supplement?* Make sure that this is firmly in the library and not the staff-room. That, at least, will make sure that all the staff come into the library!

4. Try to find time to provide the staff with some booklists, current awareness or useful topical information. This will help to raise the general profile of the library and increase your value — and by inference your status — amongst your colleagues. Never underestimate the importance of selling yourself, and your service, to your 'clients'. In any situation, it is commonplace for other people to accept the value that you put upon yourself, so be warned! If you feel you have no real role and are unappreciated and under valued, then few colleagues will see you and your library as dynamic, effective or worth supporting.

CONCLUSIONS

To sum up, then, there is no standard way in which librarians can move in order to ensure that their role, and that of the library, is one of importance and significance within the school. Each school is a separate and different community with varying objectives, aspirations and, of course, problems. Individual librarians must work within the structure that they find themselves in so it is impossible to provide a model plan or policy which would work in any given situation. What is possible is to indicate the probable steps which all school librarians must pursue in order to move along the path to a library which really does support the curriculum and is a vital part of it. Remember always:

1. Know your school! Staff, pupils, teaching methods, philosophy!
2. Understand the management structure and how you can contribute to this.
3. Look critically at how the library is seen by both teaching colleagues and pupils.

4. Evaluate the service given at present and endeavour to estimate how effective this is.
5. Probably the most important of all—be prepared for change and to abandon old ideas or routines, even if they are your special baby!

With careful and thoughtful preparation you should then be in a strong position to move on to the second stage of trying, with the help and co-operation of the head and other colleagues, to formulate a library policy. This is the very beginning of library involvement in curriculum planning and of the acknowledgement of the importance of the librarian and the library to the school.

5
Learning How to Learn: Study and Information Skills

One of the major areas where the general school curriculum meets the library is in study and information skill teaching. So much of the expertise in this subject lies with librarians as a result of their professional role and training that it increasingly makes sense for librarians to lead the development and implementation throughout the school of this vital area. In much of education, this may be thought of as a part of the secondary school curriculum and having no role in the primary school, but this is to completely misunderstand the breadth and extent of what is involved.

THE NEED FOR STUDY AND INFORMATION SKILLS

It is important to understand the reasons for the increasing emphasis placed on this area of the curriculum over the last few years for only by appreciating the need for this type of teaching for all pupils is it possible to devise an appropriate syllabus. One of the main reasons for the growth of these courses has been the change in teaching technique, and examination expectations and the gradual shift from teacher-led information to student-led independent learning. This latter fact has meant that all levels of ability are now faced not only with finding their own information but also with extracting it and presenting it in an appropriate fashion.

The advent of the CSE examination for the less able encouraged this movement and made it imperative for all pupils to be taught how to 'research' and evaluate their own information. It is probably true to say that until then it had been only the more academic pupils who were expected to be able to select and use effectively their own material. It should be noted, though, that experiments carried out on university undergraduates often showed a distressing inability to use any study or library techniques at all, so it would be wrong to assume that all the more able have an implicit understanding of these techniques and are capable of applying the right one at the right time.

On a wider front outside the school doors, there has been a massive explosion of information over the last twenty to thirty years which shows little signs of lessening. The growth of computers—and of computerised information—has been another most important aspect of this growth, and this has meant that society as a whole must be able both to understand and to make use of these facilities when necessary. Schools have in many ways led the way in realising the importance of these new skills and it is certainly true to say that, taking the population as a whole, school children are much more adept and at home with computers than many of their parents. All these factors have contributed to the growth of various schemes to teach study and library skills and have made it an increasingly important part of the curriculum in many schools.

THE AIMS OF A STUDY AND INFORMATION SKILLS PROGRAMME

There are many advantages in possessing these skills for the pupils concerned, and they are not solely concerned with better examination or test results. The aims of any programme should always include the following elements (although individual schools may have particular needs):

1. To encourage pupils to identify their needs—the analysis and definition of the questions they must ask.
2. To help pupils to make more efficient use of the resources available, including all the various selection and evaluation techniques.
3. Familiarity with quick reading aids like skimming and scanning, and also to show how to extract information from other formats like maps, graphs, etc.
4. To make pupils aware of the wide range of resources available and where they may be found. This could involve sources outside the school as well as community based information.
5. To give pupils the confidence not only to extract but also to use and present information for their own individual needs.
6. To give pupils a facility with and understanding of computerised information techniques and an appreciation of the worldwide extent of these.

7. To help pupils to develop in an intellectual and social way so that at the end of their school days they are confident about handling information and are able to operate on their own as information seekers and evaluators.

It should be noted here that many of these skills can be encouraged from a very early age and it should never be thought that study and information skills are solely part of the high school curriculum. Many succesful programmes have been mounted in primary schools which then provide a very solid basis for the more advanced work later on.

In 1981, the Schools Council produced a most useful and thought-provoking bulletin which still provides much of the basis for any study and library skills programme. The booklet was the result of a working party chaired by Michael Marland, and was meant as a practical aid to teachers wishing to do more work in this field. It attempted to tackle the vexed question of how pupils learn to learn: had the teaching of the necessary skills for this ever been part of the curriculum or, as is more likely, had many teachers simply assumed that it would happen naturally? The report noted the despair of many teachers when faced with an examination class, little if any spare teaching time, and a distressing inability on the part of the pupils either to find things out for themselves or organise effectively the information that they had found. It was obvious that such skills are not just 'assimilated' and do not happen by accident (except in very rare cases), but like all other subjects in the school curriculum need to be carefully structured and taught as part of an ongoing syllabus. Quite apart from the benefits to individual students of an increased skill and confidence in their own abilities, a properly constructed library and study skills programme can have nothing but benefits for the hard-pressed teacher. Although it may take time and effort to get such a curriculum off the ground, once established and running it should mean that all pupils become more independent and more able to operate without the full-time guidance of the teacher. This lightens not only teachers' workload but also allows them more time to concentrate on those needing more help or extra guidance, secure in the knowledge that the majority of pupils are capable of organising and completing their own work.

Research evidence has accumulated to show that the best and most effective programmes are those which involve the whole range of subjects being taught by all teachers and do not attempt to teach library and study skills as an isolated or sterile exercise. In this area it seems that 'learning by doing' is the best policy, and that the 'doing' element must not be an artificial one but must be something which pupils need to accomplish in the normal course of their studies. The best syllabus will be one which is incorporated into all the various subject departments and treats the development of these skills as a part of the normal teaching programme. Most subjects will have skills peculiar to that subject, like the interpretation of tables, graphs and statistics in economics, or the ability to 'read' information from maps in geography, and it obviously makes much more sense for these to be taught by the subject specialist as part of the everyday subject teaching. In most cases these will be already covered by the teachers concerned but probably never co-ordinated into a whole-school policy.

DEVELOPING A STUDY AND INFORMATION SKILLS PROGRAMME

It is most important that any study and library skills policy should be seen and understood by all staff as a 'whole-school policy' and not one that can be ignored or left solely to the library staff or English department. In the same way that a primary school will always have a reading curriculum and language development policy as well, so any planning for a study skills curriculum must be thought out on the same basis. A hierarchy of skills must be determined, the relevance of these to various aspects of subject disciplines calculated, and a programme worked out that takes the present and future needs of pupils into account. This should involve all heads of departments in senior schools and in smaller primary schools possibly the whole staff. It is vital for the ultimate success of the programme that all teachers feel involved and are party to the decisions taken. The leadership of this part of the curriculum should lie with the school librarian and for this they should act in a head of department capacity, co-ordinating and leading the teaching throughout the school, but relying on colleagues actually to teach specific parts of the curriculm in conjunction with particular subject or ability needs.

This latter aspect is very important and it would be a mistake to imagine that only the more academic pupils need this input. In what may seem to be a contradiction, it is possibly more vital for the lower achievers to have access to the information network at least in their own locality and to feel confident in searching out their own information. An interesting research programme a few years ago looked at the information needs of the less able and attempted to devise a teaching programme to cover them, based very much on what was of practical use to them linked to what was available locally. An interesting side-light found in this project was that although many pupils had, in theory at least, 'done' alphabetical and numerical order as part of a teaching programme on the classification scheme in their school library, few of these less able pupils were able to transfer these skills to other situations.

This reinforces the current view that teaching in this area at least must be relevant, and that exercises or instruction given purely as a 'library or study skills lesson' are at best soon forgotten and at worst totally ignored. What is taught must be part of the normal subject teaching for that pupil and relevant practice in the various skills incorporated into the work for that topic. Only then will the lessons learned be remembered, enabling the pupils to build on these skills to a greater degree of depth and complexity and subsequently transpose them to other possibly unfamiliar situations.

ORGANISING A STUDY AND INFORMATION SKILLS PROGRAMME

It is all very well knowing in theory that a study skills curriculum is a 'good thing' but quite another to actually put this into practice and have it seen by all staff and subject departments as an integral and important part of their work. Recent research amongst newly qualified teachers showed up a lack of understanding of the role of the school librarian in general and a reluctance to accept them as an equal partner in any study skills programme. If you are the school librarian, whether a professional librarian or a teacher, and interested in promoting the idea of such a scheme then there are certain prerequisites that have to be met before any real notice will be taken.

1. First the library must already have a high profile and be seen to be playing an active and important part in the school.

2. If your stock is neglected and irrelevant this is not going to inspire confidence in your abilities to lead or plan a new teaching programme.
3. The library must be open and staffed, ideally for the whole school day, but at least for a very substantial part of it.
4. The librarian must have the support of the senior staff and, most important, the approval of the head. This latter aspect is a critical factor and should never be underestimated.

To mount a successful initiative, then, you must have both a good, well run and well used library, and a supportive and enthusiastic senior management. Where do you go next?

First, look at the existing management structure within the school. What committees already exist? Is there a resource committee? Which ones do you have access to? Are you on the head of departments committee? Is there a financial group that decides money allocation (remember all new courses need resourcing with real money and pressure is always fierce for any share of this). Are there year group committees in your school, and if so, how is co-ordination achieved throughout the whole school curriculum? Your first priority must be to ensure that the library is represented in the decision-making meetings.

Once you have a plan in your mind of how power is devolved and shared in your school then you can start to make positive moves towards implementing your idea, but it will be a long hard road and no one should be under any illusions about that. Remember also that power and decision-making may not always be what they seem, and like the 'hidden curriculum' there may also be hidden power structures. These must be realised and acknowledged if anything positive is to emerge from your effort, even if this means working through the unofficial rather than the obvious committee structures.

A first step could be, after your initial enquiries, the formation of a working party or consultative group. Like-minded people would be drawn together to discuss the general idea and to canvass both opinion and options. This could become a powerful pressure group working throughout the school to get the idea discussed at all levels. A vital point to bear in mind here is to make sure that any such body is representative of the whole school, all subjects, age ranges, abilities, etc. It would be fatal to pack such a group with all the English or Arts side and ignore all the science or maths teachers. To succeed in implementing such a curriculum it must have the support of all teachers. All departments must be made to feel they have a part to play and that their subject is also one that can benefit from such a move. Never forget that you are actually asking teachers to take a further subject on board and possibly alter much of their own teaching material, or at least change the way in which they present certain elements. Try also to ensure that senior members of staff are represented on this committee as that is usually where the power lies in any school.

What should be included in any programme of library and study skills? This needs very careful thought and should not be restrictive or inflexible nor tied solely to just 'library' skills. Although the confidence to use a library catalogue or find your way around a classification scheme are important skills and should not be underestimated, it would be wrong to see these as the pinnacle of achievement. There are many other equally important accomplishments which are needed for the full development of the independent learner. Much will depend on the type of school and the age and ability levels but the elements of the programme will be similiar for all pupils involved and it is probable that modification will only be needed for certain parts. It may not seem appropriate to spend time teaching the remedial fourth year how to cope with periodical abstracts and indexes but this would be an important skill for those in the sixth form intending to go into higher education. What is included in programmes, though, must always be directly geared to work that is part of the syllabus for those pupils and can be related to their information needs. Programmes for the primary school will necessarily be simpler and, because of the different organisation within these schools, possibly easier to implement. However, what is taught there should lay the foundation for the more complicated and complex skills that will be taught later on.

A possible checklist of skills would include all the following;

1. How to organise and plan work.
2. How to find information.
3. Library user skills.
4. How to use books and other sources.
5. Skimming, scanning and other reading strategies.

6. Note-taking and note-making.
7. How to present information in differing ways.
8. Selection and evaluation criteria.
9. Self-assessment techniques.
10. Examination technique.
11. The information network.

STUDY AND INFORMATION SKILLS IN THE PRIMARY SCHOOL

For the primary school many of the skills in the checklist above are natural corollaries of much of the topic and project work that is normally an integral part of the curriculum for that age range. Looking up information, selecting the appropriate part, making notes from it and incorporating the information into the project are all very important aspects of learning and successful groundwork at an early age in these skills must give such children a head start in their future studies.

Other elements in the primary school syllabus concerned with reading and listening skills also have their part to play although this may not be so immediately apparent. The ability to search pages of text quickly for the necessary information is a skill widely practised by researchers, students in higher education and A level entrants but it is one for which the basis must be laid at an early age. Lots of practice with books in searching for 'topic' information at the junior school stage, together with skilled advice and teaching, will help to develop this as an ongoing process. The emphasis on selecting and evaluating information is again one learned initially in the earlier stages.

The practice of copying chunks from books and transferring them wholesale into the finished work is rightly deplored; exercises which make children not only select carefully what they use but also force them to write, or otherwise present it, in their own way help, to enhance and develop a selective and critical approach. Successful note-taking can be encouraged by exercises in the old English lesson of précis as well as by a variety of other means, and good listening skills may be of great importance as older pupils often need to take notes from a lesson. Pupils need to be proficient in not only hearing all that is said, but also in picking out the salient points.

In the primary school much of the work in this area will devolve upon the class teacher and an integrated and hierarchical syllabus for the whole school is the obvious approach. Many primary schools will have no central library or any sophisticated cataloguing or indexing processes and so much of the work will concentrate on encouraging the confident use of books—all the handling, reading, listening, note-taking and presenting skills, as well as the ability to handle other forms of information media like videos, computer programs, etc. Primary schools already concentrate a great deal on language, reading and comprehension skills, and these, with numeracy, lie at the heart of much of the curriculum. It is only a short step to co-ordinating and drawing together these various 'information' facets to form a whole-school curriculum. This will ensure that specific skills are included, and in the same way that other areas of the curriculum are covered during the pupil's time there, so a bank of information and study skills can also be built up.

CONTENT OF A STUDY AND INFORMATION SKILLS PROGRAMME

All schools should include the following in their syllabus, but some are obviously more appropriate for primary schools whilst others are of a more specialised nature and perhaps only necessary for the sixth form. However, high schools will need to check the ability levels of their new entrants and modify their courses accordingly. Co-operation between the feeder schools and the high school is as important in this area as in any other on the curriculum.

Alphabetical order
This seems so obvious that many teachers will give it little thought, but it is not such a simple skill as may be imagined. It is often salutary to watch an adult searching incompetently through a telephone directory and to realise that the skill needs active teaching and practice. Study and library skills, as well as such classroom activities as dictionary work, involve alphabetisation to the second and often third letters, and this is where the problem lies. Any exercises, games or practice which make this an easy and quick task will not be time wasted. As the pupils' need for more specialised information grows, so their need to use more complicated library catalogues and indexes also grows — they will then need to be proficient and adept at swift searching of alphabetical files.

It would not be difficult, at either primary or secondary level, to incorporate the teaching and practice of this into the normal curriculum. Many teachers will already accept this as a part of their syllabus, and all that may need to be done is to draw these individual strands together into an integrated, coherent and developing school plan.

Numeracy

This is so central to all education, but particularly the primary school, that it is only perhaps the emphasis necessary for the study skills element that needs stressing. Most libraries rely on a numbered classification scheme. In other words numbers are used in a code to represent subjects and the books are then placed on the shelves in numerical order, so bringing all the books on a similiar topic together. This is a simple and effective way of arranging the stock and, theoretically at least, means that anyone who can count can find the subject they want. However, the larger the library, then the more complicated and specialised the classification must perforce become, with books covered in what may appear to be incomprehensible numbers (usually in decimals)—this can be very intimidating to many adults. It can only be for the ultimate good of the pupils if they are introduced to this concept at an early age. The system is very logical and this appeals to children and makes it easy for them to understand. Practice can easily be turned into games and also made an essential part of topic or project work. Once learned, the basis of classification is rarely forgotten and can then be transferred to bigger and more complex library collections.

Reading and listening skills

Reading lies at the centre of so much primary activity and is so central to the curriculum that probably many of the reading skills needed for study skills are already incorporated into everyday practice. Skimming and scanning techniques used to search for particular items of information quickly should be part of topic and project work, and as pupils get older so the higher level evaluative and critical aspects can be introduced and practised. Listening becomes very important in the secondary school when older children may be expected to take notes in a lesson and remember the important points. Younger children can be encouraged to develop this by listening to stories and tapes and then being asked to recall them.

Book-related skills

It is very unusual to find either a child or an adult who has an instinctive understanding of how to use books in the most effective manner. Much time can be wasted by either looking in the wrong book or using it in the wrong way. Teaching in this area should start very early with simple book-handling. It is also very important to make this an enjoyable activity for primary school children as attitudes learned there will tend to follow them into adult life. The physical book will be important and time must be spent in exploring the differences, for instance, between authors and publishers, chapters and contents lists, etc. All these tasks must be carried out as part of the pupil's own 'need to know' and not taught as an isolated or theoretical skill. As students progress in the high school, so the higher level aspects such as emphasis and bias in material can be introduced as well as the principles of literature searching and the use of abstracts and indexes. What is important always is that all this must be a part of an integrated and co-ordinated package.

Library skills

Much will depend on what type or size of school you are in when planning this aspect of the programme. Many primary schools do not have any central collection or resource organisation and so any attempt to teach catalogue use or understanding of a classification scheme are bound to be a problem and could just become a theoretical exercise. Identifying and locating suitable material is an important skill and is very much tied to the use of any aids that a library may provide to help in this search. However, it is probably the older pupil, with more specialised needs, who benefits most from applying these, but, if possible, the groundwork should always be laid in the earlier years.

Note-taking and the transference of information

Extracting the relevant information and then presenting it in an appropriate way are amongst the more difficult areas for many children. Copying chunks from the first book selected is too often the response to this so much effort needs to be made to provide learners with alternative strategies and to give them lots of practice. As they get older they can then be introduced to other ways of taking notes (the spider's web technique, for instance) and presenting what they have found, possibly using other formats or technologies. What is important here is not so much which method may be chosen but that the alternatives are understood and the correct choice made.

Information technology, computers *et al*!

More and more it becomes imperative that all pupils, at whatever ability level, should leave school with both competence and confidence in handling computerised databases and all forms of information technology. This means an emphasis on retrieval methods and necessary search techniques rather than all the stress being placed on either the hardware or programming techniques. Primary school children now are all very 'computer literate' at an early age so the foundations for this particular aspect are already laid. As more high schools see computers as a normal part of their library equipment, so it should become much easier to incorporate this into the syllabus.

CONCLUSIONS

A carefully planned and implemented programme for teaching study and information skills throughout the curriculum should enable all pupils to cope with the following checklist competently and with confidence:

1. What must I do
2. Where do I go to get it?
3. How shall I find it?
4. Which resources shall I use?
5. How do I use them most effectively?
6. What records do I need and how do I make them?
7. Have I got all I need?
8. How do I present it?
9. Have I achieved all that was asked?

This list can really be used with all ages, and even young children can be encouraged to analyse and identify their needs and their work in this way.

To sum up, a curriculum that puts learning how to learn high on its list of priorities can only work to the ultimate good of the pupil and the teacher. To get such a programme off the ground needs enthusiasm, expertise and tenacity, but is well worthwhile in the end.

6
Library Routines

THE BASIC ROUTINES

It is unfortunately the case with libraries that before you can do any of the more interesting tasks, all sorts of fairly mundane and sometimes repetitive and boring jobs must be completed. The nearest analogy is the building of a house, when it is little use bothering about the state of the decoration if the foundations are likely to cave in. All libraries, of whatever type and serving whatever clientele, need a very high input of 'housekeeping', and although it is possible to cut some corners, the fundamental routines have to be carried out. These must be treated as a priority because, unless they are completed, there is no way in which the more interesting and positive work which all librarians—including those in schools—want to tackle can be sustained.

Every time a book is borrowed it needs re-shelving on its return, and every time that a book is consulted by a teacher or pupil it risks being replaced on the wrong shelf. Everyone who has ever worked in a library will know that a book misplaced on the shelf is a book effectively lost! Just keeping up with the necessary shelving and the tidying and ordering of the shelves is a very time-consuming business— and time is the one element that is missing from the timetable of virtually all teacher-librarians, many of whom are expected to teach full-time. Many professional librarians working in schools also find that their days are not long enough to fit in all the necessary tasks. Without time being given to these everyday, unglamorous and often dirty jobs, the library soon becomes untidy, tatty and eventually impossible to use effectively. Add to these essential tasks the cataloguing, classifying, compilation of a subject index, labelling and typing of cards, repairing and all the other myriad jobs and it is very obvious why many teacher-librarians (often short on experience and expertise in library skills anyway) find it impossible to cope and just give up. It is interesting to note here that so far no mention has been made for time to be allocated to book or other resource selection, liaison with other agencies, teaching or planning a library and study skills course, or work on any of the other vital areas which involve the library and the librarian in the educational work and objectives of the school.

Given that the vast majority of school librarians find themselves in this situation, and will probably continue to do so, then for the sake of self-preservation at least, it is vital to develop a strategy to enable the library to operate on as reasonable a basis as is possible in the individual circumstances. It is here that the previous formulation of clear library policy will pay dividends. This should have defined the role of the library and its long-term objectives and also have had the backing of senior management within the school. Using this document, it should be possible to draw up a realistic list of the most important tasks and also to provide justification and reasoned arguments to answer criticisms when other services are not available. Establishing the priorities is the first rule, and when time is short, making sure that these are always completed is central to good planning and will make the workload easier to bear. Obviously the size of the library and the sort of organization it needs will be determined to a certain extent by the size and type of school. It may be that in some primary schools there is no central collection at all but just a series of classroom or topic collections, whilst a big secondary school may have a large and wide-ranging collection needing a very organised approach.

THE BASIC GROUND RULES

However, whatever the particular library situation, there are certain ground rules which should apply to all libraries regardless of school or size. The important areas to concentrate on are these:

1. Creating a friendly and welcoming environment in the library. Ensure that it is a place people will come to willingly and enjoy being there. Keep it tidy (but not too like a new pin so that no one dares to touch anything) and try to make it bright and cheerful with posters, pupil's work or other 'art' on the walls.
2. Keep the rules as simple as possible and endeavour to make them positive requests rather than the very negative 'Do-not' type.

3. Remember that for many of the pupils, the school library may be the only library they ever see and so any ideas they have on libraries in general will be coloured by what they see in school. The role model of both the library and the librarian will probably remain with them, and it is important to try to leave them with a positive image to take on into their adult life.

4. Make sure that all levels of ability are welcomed into the library and that for even the slowest learners the library has something to offer. There is always a tendency to concentrate resources on the more academic and although this may be understandable, particularly when money is very short, too much emphasis here should be resisted.

5. Always bear in mind that it is no use having a marvellously catalogued or classified library with perhaps lots of computer hardware if no one feels at ease or confident in using it.

6. Encourage everyone in the school to use the library—pupils, teachers, school secretaries, cleaners, dinner-ladies, etc. Again, all this helps to promote a feeling of involvement and commitment by everyone in the school and will give many of the more reluctant pupils the role model they need to encourage them in library use. Too many school libraries still give off the aura of an academic enclave, but by encouraging *all* the adults in the school to use the facilities, much of this can be dissipated.

7. Try to make time to sit on any relevant committee, liaise with other staff and generally be in a position to represent the library and its potential for all pupils and teachers as often as possible.

These seven steps are all to do with image building and very little to do with 'library' building. However, they are probably the most important and potentially effective steps the school librarian can take to ensure that the library really is an important force within the school.

For the actual day-to-day work that running a library demands, there are some cardinal rules that should always be followed, whatever other short-cuts may be taken to reduce the workload. The important ones to remember are:

1. Have a clear idea what your final objectives for the library are and make your routines fit them—never, never do it the other way round and let the routines dictate the objectives.

2. Always make your routines as simple as possible. Keep down the bits of paper and records to a bare minimum. Ask yourself what you or other members of staff, need to know from your records and concentrate on that only.
3. Learn from other people's mistakes! Never think that it is easier to devise your own system of classification, for instance, before you have really investigated the very many pitfalls in this seemingly simple option. It is always better to stick to a tried and tested method.
4. Always be consistent, particularly in decisions to do with classification and cataloguing. Keep a record of previous difficulties you have had and follow the same rules as before. Nothing throws a user more than finding books on similiar topics scattered throughout the shelves or inconsistencies in the catalogue. It also plays havoc if the school librarian is replaced and the new incumbent has no clue as to the previous practice.
5. Make sure you know what help and advice may be available to you locally and also what you may be able to borrow from any other sources. Be prepared to call on any of these whenever you feel the need.
6. If you are new to librarianship, then invest in one or two basic books about library skills and find out what courses or in-service training you have access to. Join the School Library Association and make use of all their expertise as well as their helpful publications.

THE MAJOR PRINCIPLES OF LIBRARIANSHIP

To be confident in making decisions about what or what not to do, always remember that librarianship is based on four major principles:

1. Selection
2. Acquisition
3. Organisation
4. Dissemination

All these involve a series of sub-routines and tasks that inevitably vary in complexity depending on the type and size of library. It is obvious that a university or other highly specialised industrial library will be involved in detailed cataloguing and classification that would be in-appropriate for a school library, but the basic principle of organising the stock in such a way so that the user can readily both identify and locate required material is common to all these institutions. This is equally true for all the other three principles and the basics of librarian-ship remain the same whatever the situation.

School librarians need to break down the components of each element and then consider how important that is for the needs of their school and how high it would figure on their list of priorities, given the already stated constraints of time, energy and, probably, money as well.

SELECTION

The selection of resources for a school library involves:

1. A detailed knowledge of pupils and their various abilities, and also of teacher needs and their expectations of the library.
2. An awareness of the whole school curriculum, examination demands, special projects, special needs, etc.
3. Knowledge of present and future trends in education so that these may be taken into account in selecting.
4. Familiarity with information sources in all the physical formats and understanding of how these are used within the school environment.
5. A detailed and objective knowledge of the present stock, its problems and its gaps.
6. Knowledge of the book and resource markets and the building of a network that allows for information on new publications to be readily available, and also allows for critical and evaluative judgements to be made.
7. An ability to juggle money, organise jumble sales and hound the PTA for funds!

ACQUISITION

1. Ordering, invoicing and accounting procedures.
2. Any necessary routines to cope with chasing up late deliveries, price changes or rush order. (Some if not all of these will only refer to

the larger school library and it is unlikely that a junior school will need to set up many ordering systems apart from a straightforward record of what is on order.)

3. Checking the new stock against orders and passing the invoices for payment. If you have a poor supplier this may also entail making sure that the books you receive are in good condition and the ones you actually ordered! Some suppliers may send a delivery note and only subsequently forward the invoice so this means making sure your system can keep track of different pieces of paper arriving at different times!

4. Accessioning—that is the official taking into stock of a new item. Some schools will maintain an accession register in which all books and other resources will be entered on receipt but others may cut down the paperwork by using the catalogue to cover this function as well.

NB: This is an area which should be looked at very carefully before complex (and often duplicated) recording systems are set up. Decide what records you need, or your authority demands, and devise the simplest system you can to cope with this. There is very rarely any need in school libraries to have both a comprehensive catalogue and an accession register. Valuable time could be wasted on these double records which could be spent much more productively.

Accessioning can be very useful in a large school, or where the stock is very large, as each individual item is given a unique number which then identifies that particular book, video, tape, etc., for all time. (This unique number may also be incorporated into an issue system in some cases.) Most accession registers use the 'running number' method when the first item to be entered is given the number one, the second, two, and so on through all the stock. If you have more than one copy of the same title, the separate accession numbers can prove very useful if you want to identify a particular copy. However, this means that the order in the register is not in alphabetical, subject or any other usable order for library purposes so the accession register is very much only a backroom tool and only really of use in an accounting or inventory situation. If your authority does not demand it, think very carefully before embarking on one.

5. Labelling, jacketing and all the other clerical work connected with the physical book or resource. All libraries need to identify their own stock by some method or other and school libraries are no different in this respect. You may rely on an issue label which has the name of the school printed on it but you may also want to stamp some of the pages of the book itself for greater security. Plastic jackets, which certainly add to the shelf-life of the book, may need fitting and this latter task can sometime be fiddly and time-consuming. Many library suppliers will do this for you, although you may have to pay for this additional service. Depending on your preferred issue method, book-cards or other similiar items may need writing.

ORGANISATION

Organisation is the term used to denote not only the cataloguing and classification of the stock but also the systems such as the issue method chosen for the day-to-day administration. Included under this heading, then, are:

1. The classification of all non-fiction stock. Initially, the choice of a classification scheme has to be made, and most school libraries will turn to the Dewey Decimal Classification scheme which is the most widely used one in the country by all types and sizes of libraries. There are simplified versions aimed specifically at schools and it makes a lot of sense for a school librarian to adopt one of these. What makes no sense at all, unless you are a genius—and even then it is not to be recommended—is to try to devise your own scheme. Too many school librarians have wasted much time and effort only to discover that what appears on the surface to be a simple task is actually fraught with minefields. Before any teacher-librarian embarks on such a course, it is vital to discuss it with a professional librarian, possibly one from the School Library Service, who may be able to suggest either a different scheme or adjustments to the existing one to overcome any problems.

   Many teachers in primary schools feel that a classification scheme may be too complicated for young children to grasp but this view is not borne out by reality. Children enjoy the challenge of 'breaking the code', and this skill just needs teaching and encouraging like any other subject. Once a child can count it can use the Dewey system. The School Dewey suggests a combination of colour coding as well as the conventional classification numbers and this can certainly help with the younger children and introduce them painlessly to the concept of subject classification. Teacher-librarians, particularly, should ask for all the help they can get in both choosing and using a scheme to make sure that they do make the right decision for their situation, and so that they themselves quickly become familiar with the scheme and its operation.

2. Cataloguing is just listing what the library holds and can be as simple or as complex as the needs of the users demand. This whole area is one where the school librarian must have a very clear idea of what is needed, and an equally clear idea of what is not! Many of the older manuals on librarianship include a massive amount of detail on cataloguing and all its rules which are enough to scare any librarian away for good! Whilst it is obviously true that many large and specialised libraries must follow very precise and detailed cataloguing procedures, this is not true for most school libraries, particularly those in smaller or primary schools.

Before you embark on any catalogue at all ask yourself: What will the users ask for? If you are in a primary or junior school, or dealing with the younger age-groups in a high school, the chances are that most non-fiction requests will be subject based. A book about why birds migrate, what they wore in Roman times, or the history of transport are the sort of queries libraries in this category will tend to receive. Higher up the age group, this may start to alter and requests become much more specific. Defining the needs of your particular users at the beginning will help you to decide the really important areas to concentrate on in your catalogue and save you wasting both time and energy on making entries that will never be used.

If you are in a primary school, and time is at a premium, then make sure you have some form of subject index, but ignore the rest. You may need to provide additional information for your own use (have you already an item in stock or not?) or your colleagues, but time spent on working out an objective approach to your user needs will help you to cut down on the work and only provide what is really needed. Books of simplified cataloguing rules are available to help with difficult decisions.

The cardinal rule for both cataloguing and classification is *consistency*. Nothing is more calculated to muddle you or your users than a series of conflicting decisions about where to put different subjects or how to catalogue awkward items. Make yourself a 'rule book' and enter in it all your own solutions to particular problems —this will not only help you in the routine work but prove invaluable if you should leave and someone else takes over the library from you. Cataloguing and classification are often imbued with a sort of professional mystique, although this is not so common now as it once was. If you are not familiar with librarianship terms, do not let the jargon confuse you. Decide what you need for your library, and whatever cataloguing and classification aids are appropriate, and take all advantage of any in-service or other courses that you may have access to.

3. Issue and other control methods. It is probable that your school library will loan books to staff and pupils although there are some schools who feel that their stock is not large enough, or the security problems too great, to allow for this. This reference only approach is not a course to be encouraged and should be replaced by a loan system as soon as possible. What you decide about an issue system will again depend on the type and size of school and as a general rule, the larger the number of borrowers, then the more structured must be the system. Most schools will want answers to these questions:

- Where is a certain item?
- Who has borrowed it?
- How many items are on loan altogether?

There may be other factors that either you or other teachers would like to know—for instance, in a primary school, you may want to have a 'reading record' of books individual children borrow. The rule must always be to define what you want the system to tell you, and then choose the best option for that. Variations on the old reader's ticket and book-card abound, and possibly the best way to make an informed choice is to see as many other school libraries as possible and also to look through the catalogues from library equipment suppliers to see what else may be on offer. Larger libraries may want to incorporate refinements like a reservation system or an overdue recall, but again this will largely depend on how much time the librarian can spend and also on the degree of priority of all the options. Once more, the great advantage of having a clearly thought-out policy for the library can be of great benefit when taking these administrative decisions.

4. Libraries which have the luxury of perhaps some library assistant help or possibly parental involvement will need to organise this on a clear basis and provide a working structure which is helpful to both library staff and users.

5. Library furniture and equipment all come into this general organisation section and although funds may be very limited for this area, it should always be part of the librarian's role to know what is on offer and what would be useful in the library.

DISSEMINATION

Dissemination and exploitation of the stock are what many librarians enjoy most, although until all the previous three elements have been covered, there is little hope of indulging in this. In a school this area would cover:

1. All the teaching aspects of library use, from very simple introductions to the more complex study skills teaching. In a school situation this can be a most rewarding part of a librarian's role and lead to increased library use and a gradual progression up the skills hierarchy by all the pupils.

2. Displays, exhibitions, etc, either in the library or in various parts of the school. All these serve to highlight the involvement of the library in the school and the links with the curriculum.

3. Liaison with other organisations in the area, e.g. Museum Service, School Library Service, etc.—in fact anyone who can help with either advice or resources.

4. The encouragement of reading for pleasure throughout the school and perhaps running a school bookshop.

5. Ensuring that channels of communication are kept open with all

subject departments and interests within the school and that the library is always represented on curriculum committees and other management meetings.

6. Using all possible means to encourage and influence the setting up of a co-ordinated study and library skills curriculum throughout the school.

CONCLUSIONS

These four areas of selection, acquisition, organisation and dissemination represent the major planks of librarianship, but as in any job, the individual circumstances will alter and no hard and fast rules can be made to cover all possible situations. What is true, though, is that all libraries must contain some of all these elements to be effective and the skill of the librarian lies in determining which areas are important to concentrate on in each particular environment.

7
The Primary School Library

Like the schools themselves, primary and junior school libraries come in all shapes and sizes, and there are no hard and fast rules for their operation. However, there are two basic premises which will apply to virtually every school for children in the five to eleven age-range. The first of these is that all such schools will have a great emphasis on and commitment to language development, the teaching of reading and all the literacy skills. Most primary school teachers will see this as a most important part of their role, as well as introducing their pupils to stories and reading for pleasure. Books of all types, from the prescribed reading scheme to collections of myths and legends will play a large part in the everyday life of each class, and time will be set aside every day for reading. All these language-related skills have a very high profile in the primary school and this means that access to a wide range of reading material at all levels is of paramount importance.

It is common for schools in this category to have a language and a reading policy, either as two separate entities or, more likely, as a combined document. These will be whole-school policies which lay down a syllabus to be followed throughout all the age-ranges, and the school library and its role should certainly be incorporated into the policy. The vital and central role that the library has, not only in the encouragement of reading but also in helping to produce independent learners, should be reflected in any whole-school reading and language policy.

The second factor to be considered is that in all primary schools, with the exception of a tiny minority of very favoured ones, it will be a teacher who has to run and organise the school library, often with no free periods at all for this additional task.

WHAT MAKES A PRIMARY SCHOOL LIBRARY

The term 'library' is used here to describe the school's information resources, but in many primary schools, especially the smaller ones, there may be no central collection at all. Unlike secondary schools which have provision made in their initial planning for a library, primary schools have no such brief so there is no guarantee that a library room will be provided. It may be that a spare classroom can be turned into a library (this has become more likely recently as falling rolls have meant smaller or amalgamated classes in some schools), but often a corner of the school hall or even corridor space is used as a library. Often the library has to share its facilities with perhaps either the school television or the music room.

There will always be conflicting views over the question of a central library as opposed to classroom collections for the primary school. There is no one set of rules or guidelines to help with this decision. It will usually come down to questions of space, availability, previous practice and money, and the final outcome have very little to do with any rational discussion about the role of the library!

A centralised collection

Some of the reasons for preferring a centralised collection would include:

1. To provide for a wide range of material at all reading levels and to be able to support the curriculum by positive selection.
2. There is more control over selection and selection procedures, and it is easier to have a more objective and whole-school approach to the stock than is usually possible from the point of view of a class teacher.
3. An opportunity is provided to organise the stock in coherent and helpful manner, probably using a simplified classification scheme and some form of catalogue.
4. The chance to plan and implement a series of study and library skill lessons.
5. The gradual familiarisation of the children with the concept of a library and, over their years in the school, the opportunity to increase their confidence in handling information concepts and skills.
6. With a central collection, there is much less chance of unnecessary duplication or 'random' purchases so the money available can be spent more effectively.

7. If the school library does have a room to itself, this can be used both for 'study' purposes and, on occasions, as a quiet room.
8. Routines for such things as the control of borrowing are much simpler to devise for a central collection as it usually means that only one person is in charge, unlike a scattered collection where the school librarian may have to rely on the goodwill of individual teachers.
9. It is much easier to provide the resources for topic and project work within the school and to ensure that material on similiar subjects is provided at a variety of reading levels.
10. Expensive reference books, like atlases, encyclopaedias, etc, should always be present in any school but these need to be held centrally so that all children and staff can have access. They also cost far too much to justify any duplication.
11. A central library can provide a role model for young children if they see not only other pupils using the library but staff as well. It is not so effective if it is only one classroom and one teacher.
12. It is unlikely that more than one, or at the most, two teachers in the school will have any knowledge or expertise in library work— or even any enthusiasm for it!
13. Likewise, the school librarian will normally always be a teacher with a particular interest in children's literature, but this is not by any means true of all primary school teachers so children may suffer if no central collection (or at least co-ordination) is provided and their teacher has little or no interest or is unaware of what may be on offer.

Classroom collections

Reasons for opting for classroom collections include:

1. For young children proximity and easy access to books is very important and as few barriers as possible should be present so that they can handle and browse through books as often and as easily as they wish. No one learns to love books and reading if they can never touch them or share them with friends, and ensuring that children are surrounded by attractive books is vital for their future reading development and their education in general.
2. A too structured and 'rule-bound' central collection could deter all but the most motivated.

3. Much of a young child's growing interest in books as a source of pleasure and enjoyment comes from the enthusiasm of an adult. For the lucky ones this will probably be a parent but for many the class teacher will be the one who introduces them to the power of 'story'. For this to really work, both the teacher and the child need lots of books around them and the teacher, in particular, needs to have some control over what is available.

4. The class teacher will always have a more detailed knowledge of the children in that class and will be able to suggest suitable books for them based on both their reading ability and their known interests. Finding the right book for the right person is always important, but is even more so for early readers.

5. Any organisation of stock can be tailored closely to need and can be much more flexible.

6. Books are available throughout the school day and so none of the frustrations occur which may be present in a central collection that is only 'open' at lunchtime or break.

7. If, as is likely in most primary schools, time for the organisation and running of the central school library is virtually non-existent, then by involving all the staff in running their own class 'libraries' the load can be spread more equally.

8. Teachers are more likely to keep abreast of new books and resources if they have some responsibility for their purchase. Class libraries can encourage those who are not specially 'book-minded' to keep up to date.

The compromise situation

In the vast majority of schools, this black-and-white situation of either an organised central collection or a series of differing class libraries does not exist. Most primary schools will adopt a compromise policy that, hopefully, mixes the best of both worlds. Much will depend on space, the age of the children (is it only the sevens to elevens or are there infants as well?) and most, importantly, the interest and motivation of the head and the staff for books and libraries. There are some schools who consider that computers and videos are more important than books!

Probably the best option is a mix of both a central collection and class libraries as well. It will normally make sense to put most of the non-fiction stock into an organised, classified and catalogued (however simplified) central collection to which the whole school has access. Added to this should also be all the expensive reference material and possibly 'teacher' books as well. Class libraries would then hold most of the fiction stock of the school, together with some more general interest non-fiction, but the overall budgeting and priorities would be decided by the school librarian. The central collection would also provide for a range of fiction at differing levels so that children were not restricted to solely what was on offer in their class.

To overcome the problem of individual teachers who are neither interested in nor aware of children's literature, a system of rotating the classroom collections can be instituted. Perhaps every term the books are moved around the classes for similiar age groups, so making sure that all teachers and children have a reasonable choice.

SETTING UP THE LIBRARY

For the teacher-librarian who is faced with the task of setting up and then organising a central collection, there are certain points that need establishing and considering at the outset.

1. What is the role of the library in the school? A policy for the library and its integration into the curriculum should always be the starting point.
2. How will the children use the library? Will their visits be teacher-led or will they be encouraged to come independently to search for information?
3. How far does the school intend to go in teaching simple study and library skills?
4. How easy is it to take children to a nearby public library or will the school library have to answer all their needs?
5. Will the library be open and available for use even if no staff are present or will it only be open when you can be there?
6. How far does the physical situation of the library determine its operation (i.e. if it has to be in the school hall which may also be used for dinners and gym, then that obviously places great constraints on use)?
7. Are the books to be loaned, or is it purely a reference collection?
8. How big is the collection and how much do you envisage it grow-

ing? Remember that the greater the number of items, the more organised and structured the system to control them must be.

9. How about your own expertise and also your commitment to the job? Perhaps more importantly, how much time can you give to it?

10. What help can you expect from colleagues, either in supporting your pleas for more time and/or money, or in more practical ways with routine work in the library.

Once you have taken these decisions the other questions to do with control, routines and overall management will then raise their heads. It is true of all libraries but probably even more important for those in primary schools that the routines chosen should be as simple as possible. Anything which appears to be too complex or shrouded in mystique or lots of rules could result in many pupils being put off libraries and reading for the rest of their lives as well as giving you unnecessary work. The tragedy is that it is probably those very children who will never visit other libraries themselves or who do not see reading as a natural and enjoyable activity who will be the ones who turn away and make no effort to understand the library organisation or routines.

Teacher-librarians in primary schools should make themselves a check list of what they feel to be the most important tasks in their school and ones which provide a link between the library and teaching generally. On this list should be such questions as:

1. *What classification scheme,* if any, should be used? Unless your collection is very small indeed (two or three shelves only) then you must have some system for locating individual items and knowing what you have in stock. For most schools it is probably better to use a recognised classification scheme but in a simplified version. Coupled with this, many schools will also use colour coding which helps the younger children to find what they want and leads them naturally onto the more specialised classification numbers as they progress up the school and their needs become more specialised too.

2. *What sort of catalogue* do you need? Here you have to differentiate between the needs of the pupils and your needs as a librarian together with those of other teachers. Young children will nearly always make subject requests and when time and clerical help is at a premium, then this should be the aspect you concentrate on. Lists of subjects

with their appropriate classification number and colour will answer the vast majority of queries from pupils and you can prepare these in a number of different ways. Conventional catalogue cards can be used and filed in alphabetical order of the subject (not so easy for the little ones to use but good practice for the older ones) or posters put round the walls with the most popular topics listed. Shelf labelling is also a great help and pictures can be used to great effect to help with identification of the various topics. Perhaps you can persuade the art specialist to help — and using children's work is always a good ploy as it will give them a feeling of involvement.

For your own needs, you may need to consider an author or title file, otherwise it is going to be impossible to check your stock and know what you have. Much will depend on what records you keep of your orders, whether you have an accession register and how big your stock is. If you have the time, then an author and title file will help not only you and the other staff, but also introduce the children to more detailed search procedures. If you opt only for the subject index, then real problems arise with the fiction stock as here most children will make either title or author requests. Again, your approach for practical solutions to these questions will be determined by your knowledge of your school, the teachers and the children, and your own expertise and time available.

3. *Issue methods* vary greatly and some involve much more work than others. Again, your first decision will be whether to loan books at all. Even then you may be faced with a variation on this when books may be allowed into the classrooms but not out of the school. All these considerations will influence your choice so it is vital to settle these before you decide on the system.

The other aspect to consider in a school is how much you would wish to follow the individual children's reading choice or whether you are more interested in how often a book is borrowed rather than who borrows it. Methods vary from a tatty exercise book written in by pupils or teachers when something is borrowed, often illegible and proving impossible to pin-point a particular item, to very sophisticated copies of the systems used by public libraries. These usually involve lots of tickets, book-cards, labels and other paraphernalia which are very expensive both in terms of the time needed for administration and in money to provide all the stationery. Young children (and adults as well!) find it all too easy to lose library tickets and all sorts of confusions can result when these are used by other people.

Look at what other schools do, ask other teacher-librarians, and get ideas from the catalogues of some of the major library equipment suppliers. These latter will normally be held by your nearest School Library Service or large public library. Make the system you choose fit what you need to know and that you know you can cope with.

The basic intent behind all these decisions is to make you think out very clearly what you and your users want out of the system, and then to opt for the least time-consuming routine that is commensurate with those needs.

Other potential problem areas could include some or all of the following:

1. Inheriting, as a new school librarian, an ill-assorted, badly organised collection of resources. If this happens to you, before processing any stock, go through it very carefully and select only those items which you feel will be used and are relevant to your needs. Discard all dirty and torn material and take as your guide the question 'Would I borrow this from a public library?' If the answer is in the negative, then on no account hang onto the book. Children should not be expected to use materials which are below an accepted standard.

2. Books that really belong in the library but are tucked away in teachers' stock cupboards. This problem may have arisen in the past when teachers felt that the library was not secure and so books were lost, or that they themselves found access difficult so built up their own private library. Either way. the result is to weaken the central stock. Tact, perseverance and proving that the library is efficient are probably the best weapons to use to remedy this.

3. A book-stock that may favour one age group or subject area to the detriment of others. This may mean buying heavily into other areas to redress the balance—a policy that may not be understood by some other teachers.

4. One of the most difficult problems to tackle is when the library is virtually ignored by other members of staff and only lip service is paid to it. There is no easy solution to this, and a long-term cam-

paign will have to be waged to change attitudes. This will probably include trying to involve the staff in book selection for their age groups or pet subjects, working hard to establish the curriculum links and generally raising the profile of the library by all possible means.

5. Money problems are probably endemic for most school librarians but sometimes the primary school librarian has other problems to overcome. Heads have been known to spend all the school's book allowance without consulting the librarian and to fill the library with what may seem tempting 'remainder' bargains but which in reality are little use. Again, this will only be solved by the persistence and tact of the librarian and by trying slowly to educate the staff and the head in the art of evaluative and critical book-selection.

CONCLUSIONS

Primary school libraries are really little different in essence from their larger high school counterparts. Where they do have much more influence is in their role in promoting reading for pleasure as well as for information. It is a potential not to be squandered.

8
The Secondary School Library

Over the years, secondary school libraries have always received much more attention than their primary counterparts. This has not been altogether unreasonable given that virtually all secondary schools have had some form of library provision, however low the standard, and always had some member of staff designated as the school librarian. This has often involved an additional salary scale and been, in a sense, part of the school's established staffing structure. Whether this person is a professional librarian as opposed to a teacher-librarian is a fairly recent development, but it would be unusual to say the least to find a secondary school where no such post was even listed, even if, in the event, only lip service is paid to the whole concept of school libraries and librarians.

From the beginning of this century when the Building Regulations for schools included a special library room for all high schools, the emphasis in various official publications has been very much on the needs of the older pupil. The School Library Association itself was founded by teachers working in secondary schools and it was not until about thirty years ago that the SLA paid much attention to the younger age-group. The Library Association also followed this pattern and in their standards they also concentrated on this area of work. Much of the present day debate about the role of the school library, its links with the curriculum, examination demands and library and study skills courses all reflect the interests and needs of the older pupils rather than the younger children. As with primary schools, the variation in the standard of provision in secondary schools is huge, ranging from very well-stocked and organised collections that resemble small branch libraries in the services and facilities offered to a tatty, irrelevant and ignored library that is like a jumble-sale collection more than anything else. What does mark the secondary school out is that it will nearly always have a room designated as a library and furnished as such. This is not to say that it will always be used as such, and many libraries double as classrooms or are reserved exclusively for the sixth form study area. But, somewhere in each school, there should exist—in theory at least—a library room.

FUNCTION OF THE SECONDARY SCHOOL LIBRARY

What differences are there, or should there be, between libraries that cater for the younger children and those for older students? The basic answer is that the foundations of librarianship are the same in whatever situation, but that the dove-tailing of these to user needs is where the art of the librarian lies. Selection, acquisition, organisation and dissemination are still the principles by which all librarians work and do not differ fundamentally wherever the library.

These main areas must always be covered, but in addition, school libraries have other roles to fulfil. In 1972, the School Library Association said that a school library should fulfil three main functions:

1. As a place of reference to answer specific queries and provide information.
2. As a place of study where individuals can work independently.
3. As a place for recreational reading and where the pleasures of reading can be enjoyed and promoted.

In the late 1980s these are still very important aims but most school librarians would want to expand and add to this list. The list now should read more like this:

1. To provide the school with a centralised resource covering all types of materials.
2. In conjunction with this, to contribute to the school the experience and expertise of a librarian and all those skills associated with this.
3. To both lead and influence the positive links between the curriculum and the library.
4. To establish a whole-school policy for the teaching of library and study skills.
5. To encourage the concept of independent learning as a life-long skill.
6. To promote pleasure and enjoyment in reading.

7. To introduce all pupils to the whole field of information technology
   and ensure that they are all competent practitioners in retrieving
   information by these means.
8. To provide staff with suitable material for their needs.
9. To liaise with all other relevant organisations.

Most high school libraries will be much bigger than those in primary
schools and will probably have not only a much larger stock but also
a more complex one covering many subjects at a great variety of levels.
This means that the structures and routines for the library must be
carefully thought out and tailored to the more specialised needs of both
the users and the stock.

SELECTION

No one person, however motivated or well-trained in selection criteria,
can be an expert in every subject, and the more specialised the topic,
then the more difficult materials become to assess. In high schools this
becomes increasingly difficult as resources for the older pupils are
chosen. It means that school librarians must be aware of a very wide
range of information sources on new books and other materials, and
they must also build up a network within their schools of specialists in
various subject disciplines who will not only assess individual items but
also suggest and monitor their own particular area. High school selection also implies a detailed knowledge of the curriculum as it applies
to all ages and levels of ability together with an awareness of national
trends in education and changes in, for instance, examination
syllabuses. It is also very probable that high schools will use a substantial amount of non-book material both in the classroom situation and
also for independent study. This means a familiarity with video,
cassette, computer programs, etc, and how they will be used within the
school, as well as the often very difficult task of how to locate individual
items and where to track down any reviews of them.

Periodicals will also be an important element in high school libraries,
although shortage of funds raises great problems for the supply of these.
Schools often have to rely on members of staff passing on their own
copies of magazines. Whilst this can be very helpful it has two major
disadvantages. First, the supply may dry up if the teacher either leaves

or cancels the subscription, and secondly it leaves the school librarian with only minimal control over what may be on offer. For pupils going on to higher education, it is very important that they should have access to periodical literature and begin to understand the central role it has in academic work.

A further problem that may affect selection in high schools is communication. Many have very large staffs, some are on split sites and others have similar logistical problems, all of which make it difficult actually to talk to other members of staff and establish any rapport with them. If time is also at a premium then the problems are compounded and even trying to keep abreast of change and development within the school may not be possible.

ACQUISITION

Routines for this area will probably have to be more structured than for smaller primary or middle schools as both the amount of stock involved and its compexity will inevitably mean more administration and more paperwork. There will also, hopefully, be more money available for the purchase of books and materials, so a record system will have to be set up to account for this and a more detailed note of orders, receipts, and invoices, etc., instituted.

Again because of the greater size of the library, probably more clerical work will be involved in processing the actual books and other resources. Labels, school stamps, jackets as well as possibly book-issue cards will probably need preparing for all new books, and the non-book material will also have to have some permanent form of identification. This latter can sometimes be quite a problem and special equipment may sometimes be needed to cope with videos or computer programs. For larger libraries, an accession register will probably always be necessary, and there may be other accounting or inventory routines to complete that either the school or the LEA insist on.

ORGANISATION

Both the classification and the catalogue will have to be quite detailed and more initial thought given to choosing the right scheme. Once a large collection is established and organised on any basis, it is virtually impossible to alter this as the time is never available for any retrospective classification or cataloguing. This makes it imperative that the correct system is chosen from the outset. The rule to remember is that the chances are that the collection will grow, so whatever the decision, what is chosen must be capable of expansion and coping with an increase in stock and use. What works for a very small collection with few borrowers will not necessarily cope if the situation alters. Although, again, simplicity for both user and librarian should always be one of the elements, it has to be balanced by the realisation that too simple a system could store up trouble for the future.

It is more than likely that most schools will adopt one of the major classification schemes. This will probably be the Dewey Decimal Classification scheme. It has the big advantage of being widely used in most public libraries as well as many other types of library and has a number of differing editions, from the full version with all the more specialised classification numbers included, to the very simple editions which are useful to schools and other libraries where a high degree of differentiation is not so necessary. The School Library Association has produced, in conjunction with the American publishers of Dewey, an edition specially aimed at British schools and this would be a useful starting point for teacher-librarians, particularly those who have had no previous experience in classifying. However, if your library is very large and contains much specialist material, then you will probably need one of the larger versions. Take advice from your School Library Service or from other school librarians in similar schools.

The catalogue will also need to be a more complicated and structured affair allowing for users to access information from it by various routes. The main points to cover will be the following:

1. Has the library a book by a certain author?
2. What has the library on a particular topic or subject?
3. Has the library a book with a particular title? (This is more necessary for fiction than non-fiction.)
4. If the item is not a book, but perhaps a video, then the entry must make this plain, and possibly show additional details such as location if it is housed in a separate place or it it needs particular hardware to use the item.

The individual entries in the catalogue must also contain considerably more information than is necessary in primary schools and all the following items could be important depending on the particular school, its philosophy and teaching methods. Bear in mind that a school that is encouraging a high degree of independent learning, using any resource-based learning techniques and, as all schools will be now, involved in the GCSE syllabus, will need a libarary and resource base to provide the foundation for this type of work and so the demands on the libarary will be greater. Your catalogue entries may therefore need some or all the following:

1. The author and title statements together with publisher and date of publication. This latter will be important particularly in science and technical fields although you may decide that you do not need to know the publisher. This fact can be helpful, though, both to the librarian and to other teachers, as the reputation of particular publishers in certain areas can tell you something about the authority of the book.

2. Subject entries so that users who may not know of any specific book can find out quickly and easily what the library holds on any topic.

3. Edition number is specially important for all books and materials in the scientific and technical fields, and also for any annual publications or in such areas as the social sciences and welfare where legislation may alter from year to year.

4. The presence in the item of illustrations, maps, graphs, etc. This may be useful for some of your enquirers to know before they actually search for the item on the shelves.

5. If the item is not a book but a video, cassette or other format, then the entry must make this quite clear and give additional information about where the item is housed and also if it has any special considerations (e.g. VHS or BETA video?).

6. Most important for all entries, where the item can be found. This may be a simple classification number, or in schools on a split site or with other logistic or storage problems a room location. The entry must make it quite clear to the user where to go to retrieve the sought item.

7. Series entries are sometimes found useful by teachers, but before you embark on doing them, be quite sure that the result is worth

the effort. For most pupil users this entry will mean little and in most cases involve much extra work for no good purpose.

8. Accession number, if an accession register is kept. It is a useful check on items to note the accession number on the catalogue card as this is a unique number and will only apply to that one item. However, make sure that if this number does appear on the catalogue card that there is no danger of users confusing this with the classification number.

9 Number of copies as often a school library will buy more than one copy of much used texts. It is always useful to have this recorded on the catalogue entry together with the individual accession numbers if such a register is kept.

There are cataloguing rules and simple books to help those inexperienced in this field, but again, the cardinal rule must be to define very clearly what the needs of the users are and plan your strategy accordingly. Many cataloguing guides will list an extensive and, to the lay person, complicated set of rules for catalogue entries. Whilst it is certainly very important indeed to be consistent and follow a laid down set of rules, there is no law which says you should follow slavishly every rule in the book. Choose those that are important in your situation and be careful and consistent in following them. Advice from other teacher-librarians—and also learning from other people's mistakes—can be a help. There are different ways of designing a library catalogue which can affect how it is used. Read a simple explanation of these alternative filing systems and ask around before you embark on one or another. Whatever you choose, it will involve you in a considerable amount of both the professional library work of cataloguing and the clerical work of typing and filing.

Entries also have to be kept up to date and this means removing entries for stock that is lost or withdrawn as well as preparing all the new cards. The advent of computers in school libraries is not likely, in the near future at least, to affect this procedure drastically. Although large libraries have computerised catalogues, this is not by any means a cheap option and it is unlikely that many schools will be able to afford or even justify the expense. It also needs considerable computer expertise on the part of the school librarian in both selecting the hardware and a suitable software package. There may be possibilities for computerisation, even if of only some of the stock, if your school is part of a computer network and the work and the results can be shared. To give pupils experience of computer catalogues some school librarians have opted to select a topic and put all the material on it onto a computerised database. This has the great advantage of not stretching too much the resources of the librarian in terms of both time and money, and allowing students to learn how to access such information both on an independent basis and by more structured teaching in a study skills curriculum.

DISSEMINATION AND EXPLOITATION

This is probably the area of work that any librarian enjoys most, and school librarians are no different. This is the work that is actually done with the users to help them and to encourage them to become independent searchers for information. It embraces all the various study and library skills techniques as well as the 'public relations' aspects of making sure that the library is represented on school committees and shows a high profile throughout all the school. In school librarianship, this part of the work places great emphasis on the teaching aspects and ensures that the curriculum links are not only present in theory but work in practice. It is really the total involvement of the library in all aspects and areas of the school's work.

PROBLEMS FACING SECONDARY SCHOOL LIBRARIANS

High school librarians often have to grapple with a range of difficulties, some or all of which may be present in any school.

Staffing
High schools in some parts of the country are fortunate in having a full-time professional librarian on their staff whose sole function it is to organise and manage the library. For these schools, this means that the library can be open at all hours, it has someone who should be quite objective about both the stock and the library's needs and there is someone always on hand with appropriate expertise to help all users. In these cases, the library will probably be very well classified and catalogued as well as kept tidy with the shelves in order. The librarian

will know all the main sources of information on new materials and be able both to suggest and direct teachers to new information. Probably most importantly of all, the professional librarian will not be faced with split loyalties between the demands of a heavy teaching timetable and the needs of the library. (Inevitably in this conflict, the library nearly always loses out.) Teacher-librarians also face the equally difficult problem of their own role perception and often find it hard to handle these two roles and present to other members of staff a positive view of the library.

It has been noted earlier that professional librarians can run very efficient and effective school libraries, although their lack of an educational background sometimes, inevitably, places them at some disadvantage. Teachers with some training in basic librarianship skills and with the time allowed for library work that professional librarians receive may have more chance of integrating the library whole-heartedly into the curriculum and gaining the co-operation and trust of their teacher colleagues. The ideal, of course, is a dually qualified person but this is very rarely realised.

Clerical help is another bugbear for nearly all librarians, whether teachers or professionals. Some schools are lucky in having some typing assistance for the library, but in most cases it means either doing it yourself or having very good relations with the school's secretarial staff. Either way, it is very time-consuming and can mean that other work has to go by default.

Accessibility

Accessibility to the library really goes hand in hand with staffing. If the school has no full-time librarian or, more rarely, library assistant help, then the library may be seldom open. Some schools feel that it is not safe to leave the library unlocked and unattended as too much stock may disappear without trace. This is an understandable worry but does mean that genuine users cannot gain access when they need to and, through sheer frustration, begin to ignore the library as an information source altogether. The other pattern that also often emerges in this situation is that staff build up their own little subject 'libraries' which are scattered around the school in stock cupboards with no central record of who has what!

All this has a snowball effect: as demand falls off, the case for both resources and staff becomes harder to justify and the library gradually becomes a neglected, unloved and underused area of the school with little or nothing to show how it could operate under different circumstances. Very serious thought should be given before a library is locked and access denied for much of the time as the repercussions could be much greater, and potentially more damaging, than the possible loss of some stock.

Space constraints

Sixth-form study and other space demands can also be a serious problem in many high schools. If the sixth form with the large number of private study periods that is usual at this level, have no particular place to work, then the library will seem to many in the school—teachers as well as the sixth-formers themselves—the ideal place. It is an argument difficult to refute but it can mean that other pupils are discouraged from using the library, and the less able may feel particularly vulnerable if the more academic A-level students are always around. The presence of the sixth form in the library may also make it impossible to conduct any sort of library or skill lesson there for other groups. However, the positive side of this could be that the sixth form could be encouraged to provide some mild form of supervision so keeping the library open when no staff are available.

Schools with space difficulties may also decide to take over the library as additional classroom space and again, short of lying down by the door and refusing entry, there is little the school librarian can do. The 'sin-bin'syndrome can be a futher problem in some schools with the library used for recalcitrant pupils who have been banished from the classroom. This does nothing for the library's image, except in a very negative way, and should be strongly resisted.

Falling rolls have helped in some schools to overcome the pressure for space but in the last analysis it is the role of the library in the school which will be the determining factor. The perception of the library by other teachers, but particularly by the head and top management, is central to this as well as to the related staffing and resource provision issues. A library that is held in high esteem by all staff and pupils, that provides an effective and meaningful service to all its users and is in the forefront of leading the teaching in both library and study skills as well as the new information technology, is unlikely to be threatened by a 'takeover'.

THE IMPACT OF GCSE

GCSE will have a great impact on the role of the library in the school, although as things appear at the moment, little thought or, even more important, finance has been given on a national level to this aspect of the new examination. Librarians are well aware of the implications for resource provision within the school that this new syllabus will entail but few LEAs have as yet made any real attempt to deal with this problem. Many of the criteria laid down by the Secretary of State for GCSE include assessment objectives such as the following:

1. Gathering and ordering relevant information;
2. Evaluating reading material;
3. Selecting suitable sources from a wide range of possibilities;
4. Presenting effectively the sought topic;
5. Analysis and critical evaluation of information presented in a variety of formats.

These are just some of the main objectives of the new syllabus—within each subject area will be found more detailed and explicit guidelines for pupil achievement, and most of these will have at least an element which demands of the student some independent study and evaluation of material. Schools which already have well-stocked and organised libraries with positive curriculum links are obviously going to be at a great advantage in preparing their pupils for GCSE. The role of the librarian, and his or her expertise in information selection and retrieval, is central to much of the teaching here and schools that do not have access to this expertise will find their task in preparing students so much more difficult. Inevitably, those LEAs or individual schools which have already taken the initiative in this library provision will be the winners, and schools—too many of them—which have no real working library but only lip service paid to the concept will be the losers. More important, their pupils will be at a grave disadvantage compared with their peers from other schools.

With the benefit of hindsight it is now possible to appreciate how central to the future role of the school library was that most valuable document *School Libraries: The Foundations of the Curriculum.* All that was contained in there has been reinforced by the recent statements made about this new examination structure, but if this is to work as the DES would wish, then the school library and school librarian, whether teacher or professional librarian, must be heavily involved.

CONCLUSIONS

Trends in education, for high schools at least, would seem to indicate an increasing role for the information expert. The involvement of the specialist in this field, the librarian, is vital as the skills of librarianship are more and more in demand. Secondary school librarians can have great influence over the intellectual development of all the pupils in a school, and not only give them a lasting love of books and reading, but an enthusiasm for seeking out knowledge and the ability to carry this out for themselves.

9
Book Selection: The General Principles

It is all too easy to waste money on books and other resources. Unlike many other commodities, it is not true of books that you get what you pay for and some expensive books certainly do not justify their high price. It is not difficult, even sometimes for the experienced buyer, to pay out hard-won money for rubbish, or at best something that does not quite do what you want. The increase in the number of books published each year shows little sign of slowing down and it is impossible for anyone to keep abreast of them all, or even to read the major reviewing periodicals. It is particularly difficult for the teacher-librarians for two reasons. First, their time for the library is usually very limited and even keeping up with the day-to-day routines becomes a never ending struggle. To add to this more time and effort in trying to find out what is new and relevant to the school library is an extra burden which many of them find impossible to carry. Their second problem is that, in the main, they do not have the knowledge of the book and related information world that is a normal part of most librarianship training and subsequent professional expertise. Librarians are trained to know their sources and to be able to identify quickly the important features. They also have specific training in selecting materials and in assessing and comparing items. In the school situation, they also have more time to give to this important element of their work than do their teacher-librarian counterparts.

GENERAL CRITERIA FOR BOOK SELECTION

However, there are ways to make the task easier and more effective whatever your previous training or your present position. Needs will vary according to the particular school, its intake, examination syllabus, general reading levels, etc, but included on all school librarians' selection checklist should be the following:

1. Know and understand the role of the library in your school. How far is it tied to the curriculum? How much is it used for recreational reading? What about teachers' use or the library's own teaching role? There may well be other considerations in your school to take into account but these are some of the basic questions which may determine your buying priorities.

2. Know your own stock intimately—its gaps, its needs, what is popular and well used and what sits on the shelf doing nothing. This is probably a more reliable guide to what you should be buying than many other more theoretical guidelines. The stock use in your own school library should largely reflect your user needs and this should help you to buy sensibly and to concentrate on material that you are confident will be used. Know, also, what is needed for particular courses, changes in curriculum or examinations. Try to look at the stock quite objectively and endeavour not to let bias or overstocking in any special area creep in.

3. Bear in mind what kind of library you have in school. Is it one central collection, or is it scattered throughout classrooms or split between different sites? In either of these two circumstances you may need to consider duplication of certain items.

4. Talk to colleagues about their information needs and those of their pupils, and also use their knowledge of what is available in their subject fields. However, guard against very enthusiastic teachers trying to fill the library with their own special topics, and balance what they can tell you with what you already know about your stock.

5. Is yours a lending library and can pupils take books home as well as use them in the classrooms? Demand will vary depending on such factors and you need to be aware of this.

6. Know your own local resource 'network'. What can you borrow from other sources and under what circumstances? This will probably mean initially your local School Library Service and all the services that may offer, but it may also include the Museum Service, the local teacher's centre, possibly the local public library and any special arrangements it has for teachers, and any other sources you know about. If you can borrow material that is only rarely used or only needed for a 'one-off' project, then there is little point in spending the book-fund on it.

A second strand to this resource knowledge is to be aware of where else pupils may go for their information or recreational needs. If you have a good library near to you, then that can probably offer pupils a reasonable choice of at least recreational reading so leaving you freer to concentrate on the curriculum demands in the school library.

7. Always make stenuous efforts to see the book or other material before you buy. This may not be at all easy. Much will depend on where you live, on how efficient your local School Library Service may be, and perhaps on whether you are close to a good bookshop or to a library supplier. It is, though, a cardinal rule to see before buying if at all possible.

If your authority is part of a central purchasing group, then they may offer a 'bookshop' or other previewing facility. If you cannot see any item, then do at least try to read as many reviews as possible. Most schools will take at least *The Times Educational Supplement* and most of the major educational materials will be reviewed in this. The School Library Service in your area will take all the other major reviewing periodicals and more than likely make them available to anyone interested. Some areas will have their own locally produced reviewing magazine and this can be of particular use as local teachers and librarians who have done the reviews can be easily contacted for more information.

The nearest large public library, particularly one with a large reference department, will also take a very wide range of periodical literature, and if you are lucky to have a university, polytechnic or college near to you, then the chances are that they will also have a large stock. Although they may not grant you 'borrowing' rights, they will probably be happy for you to read the magazines *in situ*.

The School Librarian, the quarterly journal of the School Library Association, is also very good value as not only does it have a substantial review section written and geared for teachers, librarians and pupils, but also interesting and informative articles about the whole field of school librarianship.

8. Never forget that publishers' catalogues are basically a selling and advertising medium and that they are quite specifically designed to encourage you to buy their product. The information in them is carefully written to produce the effect that the publisher wants

(in other words—sales!) but it will not necessarily tell you what you need to know. Treat all such publications with a reasonable degree of cynicism—even the more well-known names in publishing need to keep up their sales figures as well! However, publishers' catalogues are very useful for telling you what is new on the market, who has written a new book and what else is coming in a popular series. As a source of initial book information, they are very useful and all libraries should always hold an up-to-date file of them. You may also need them to supply the bibliographical details of price, ISBN etc., that you may need for ordering any item.

9. Do not buy, unless you are very sure of your ground, from a publisher's representative or other 'bookseller' who calls on the school. As with the catalogues, remember that these people are employed to sell and are often very highly trained in selling techniques. It is very important to bear in mind that, however impressive a particular book or other item a representative produces is you have not seen any of the other comparable offerings from other firms or sources. Your finances probably mean that you can only buy one, or at the most two items on this topic at this level. If you only see what one publisher is offering, how can you judge it? It can be a very instructive exercise to collect together a number of books on the same topic and try to decide on a 'best buy'. The differences can be immense and price is usually no indicator of worth.

If you are in a primary school, then you may have a further problem to face over representatives calling on schools. It will normally be the head who sees the caller whilst you may be in your class and quite unaware that the head has spent half your treasured book-fund on materials you do not want. This has been known to happen and is very difficult to counter, but again, the higher the profile that the library holds in the school, the less likely this is to occur. In most secondary schools, particularly those with a professional librarian, this will probably not occur as the representative will wish to see the school librarian rather than the head and make arrangements to do so.

10. Be wary of publishers' series. Some of these are very good and have rightly earned themselves a high reputation. Some, though, are again just selling ploys where the publisher hopes to persuade you

to buy further books on the basis of earlier successes but with little or no evaluation of the latest offerings. Many series, particularly at the younger end of the market, are just packaged in a similiar way and their contents can vary enormously.

11. Inspection copies that publishers offer to schools can be another minefield unless you are very strong-minded. In theory it does seem a good idea to take advantage of this service to look at possible books prior to purchase but the problem lies in the return of unwanted items. It is just so much easier to pay the invoice and keep the book rather than pack it up, post it and return it. This is really a form of 'inertia' selling and should be recognised and treated as such. By all means look at all the books you can, by whatever means possible, but do not be persuaded into buying books you are not really sure about or cannot compare with similiar offerings.

12. There will always be the question of replacement to consider, either of lost items or ones that have fallen to pieces through intensive use. Some portion of your money will have to be allocated to renewing your important items and this must be taken into account in any budgetary decisions.

13. Last, but by no means least, how much money have you to spend and how long has it to last? Some school libraries will be given an annual sum whilst others may be doled out odd sums on an *ad hoc* basis. This money supply problem can affect the buying policy very much (in fact in the worst cases make it virtually impossible to have any policy!) and it is sometimes difficult to stick to a logical and coherent plan. Most school librarians, and teachers in general, can remember occasions when a sudden glut of money had to be spent in a tearing hurry with no time for forethought, or the opposite when expected funds did not materialise. It behoves all school librarians to keep an ongoing list of both subject gaps and specific titles to cope with these sudden fluctuations.

SPECIFIC CRITERIA FOR BOOK SELECTION

Following on from these points of a more general nature, there are a series of more specific criteria to look for in all books. Some of these will vary depending on the school, the users and the needs but in general most will apply to the majority of situations and can, anyway, be adapted to special circumstances.

Non-fiction

The criteria for assessing non-fiction will include:

1. Is the text accurate? This is not always easy to judge, particularly in any specialist areas, and you may need to find someone who understands the topic to give you an opinion. Here, authoritative reviews will help as will the reputation of the author and the publisher. It is obviously important to make sure that you are not unwittingly peddling suspect facts, especially as for many pupils the school library may be their only source of information. Some junior non-fiction has had a rather poor reputation for producing 'scissors and paste' books—in other words someone has some pretty illustrations and someone else, who is not necessarily an expert on that topic, is asked to write an accompanying text. The resulting hotch-potch may be packaged attractively and unsuspecting teachers and librarians will buy it, but it may be that the content is not of the standard you would wish so beware of this essentially 'marketing' ploy.

2. A corollary of this is to try and check what may be left out of a book. Does it give as clear, unbiased and full picture of what it purports to be about, commensurate with the age-range for which it is intended? For instance, you may find, particularly in older history and geography books, that they give a very eurocentric view of development. The facts as stated may be quite correct but it could be that the omissions cause the book to be unbalanced.

3. Is the writer enthusiastic? Non-fiction often suffers from the 'hack-writer' syndrome and this is particularly true of children's non-fiction. When a book is written by someone who has a real desire to share their interest with the reader, then that book stands out from the rest.

4. Does the book stimulate thought and discussion? This is really a direct follow-on from the previous point, as most enthusiastic authors do have this affect. There will always be some books that do not pass this test but which you need to stock—the more factual and reference books for instance, but do look for these special ones.

5. Are fact and opinion clearly differentiated? This can cause problems for younger children who are still learning to select and evaluate their own information. It may also need thought when purchas-

ing books for the older pupils where possibly social, political or economic topics are concerned.

6. If the book is illustrated, how much does this add to the understanding of the text? Do these two elements appear to be two halves of one whole or two completely separate entities?

7. The illustrations should always be at a similiar conceptual level to the text. It can happen, particularly in the 'scissors and paste' type of publication where little co-operation has been possible between author and illustrator, that there is a discrepancy and a mismatch here.

8. The younger the child, the more important becomes the reading level, although this is also vital for the slow learners in high schools. Authors and publishers who understand the demands of both conceptual and reading levels and can marry these to the needs of teachers and education are to be cherished!

9. Check the type size and the physical design of the book. The type size is very important for younger or poor readers, and how the illustrations and text are arranged on the page can help or hinder the less confident.

10. How easy is it for the readers to find their way through the book? What 'aids' does it have to help in this? Index, contents list, glossary, chapter headings, etc., are all very helpful. If you are assessing a book that is obviously aimed at project work or other independent study, then the book itself should help the user to find specific information and not involve him or her in reading through all the text to find one fact.

11. For the younger age-group in particular, it is important to check how quickly new ideas and concepts are introduced. Is it a logical step-by-step sequence or does the book assume too much too quickly?

13. The physical characteristics and durability of the book are important in any library situation, and especially when money is tight these cannot be ignored. The book must be capable of standing up to a reasonable amount of wear and tear, and not always of the more careful kind. This sometimes makes librarians very wary of paperbacks or other more 'ephemeral' types of pulishing, but experience in many libraries has proved that, if paperbacks are fitted with plastic jackets, their shelf-life is as good. As they are so much

cheaper than a hardback, they are therefore often much better value for money. Many more titles can be bought and more variety provided than would be possible with a policy of hardback alone. Do not let the physical aspect be too high on your list of criteria—it is a consideration, but a book that you feel will really fill a gap in your stock should never be ignored purely on physical grounds.

14. A final point to check in all resource material must be to look carefully and see if it could be offensive or hurtful in any way to any group or race (see below).

Fiction

Many of the points made above for non-fiction selection are equally valid when choosing fiction, but there are some additional checks to bear in mind:

1. Is it a story your pupils will want to read? However meritorious the author or high the 'literary' merit of the book, if no-one wants to read it, it is a waste of money. This is not to say, though, that all standards should be thrown out and a diet of trash and comics provided. The art of good selection, especially in school libraries, is to balance the interests and abilities of the pupils with your knowledge of what exists in the market, and to try to provide stimulating, well-written stories that they will enjoy reading.

2. Much of the adult 'lit.crit.' criteria can equally well be used with all fiction for whatever age. Are the characters stereotyped? Do they grow and change throughout the book? How do you rate the writing style? Is there language enrichment for your potential readers?

3. What will it do for developing the imagination of your readers? Will it help them both to understand themselves and other people?

4. Check that the theme, the language used and the reading level are all right for the intended readerhip—this is by no means always the case.

5. Look for any offensive or hurtful passages. This can be a problem particularly in reprints of children's stories originally published either before the last war or just after. Attitudes and perceptions, particularly over race, were very different then and stocking some of these now can raise delicate issues. (See further below.)

6. If it is an historical novel, or any other particular setting has been used, try to ensure that this is accurate.

7. Again, look at the physical book, but never discount material just for this. In junior fiction, particularly, there is a wealth of choice in paperback and this is usually very popular with users.

OTHER CRITERIA FOR BOOK SELECTION

There are four other areas which, although part of the more general criteria, also have more specific importance attached to them. These concern picture books for young children (although these will really only concern those teachers in primary schools), race, gender and other contentious material.

Picture books for primary children
The main points to watch out for are as follows:

1. Look for picture books where the artistic quality is high but beware of the 'trendy' picture books which bear more relation to an art student's portfolio than to any real understanding of what young children enjoy and can appreciate and understand.
2. Try to ensure that it is a 'whole' book and not two disparate halves of text and pictures. Some of the best books for this age range have been produced by one person doing both parts but look also for some of the successful collaborations between artist and writer.
3. How far will the pictures help to make the text more understandable? Remember that many of the 'readers' will still be at the very beginning of decoding print and often not even at that stage. Good illustrations will not only add to the story but help to tell it as well.
4. Will the book give anything to the child's visual perception and artistic sense? Is the text well written or is it just a rather trite vehicle for the artwork?
5. Is there lots to look at and talk about in the pictures? This is very important as for many young children the power of imagination, sense of story and language development are all encouraged by exposure to a wide variety of picture books.
6. Most importantly, do the writer and illustrator understand the interests, concerns and curiosities of the young reader and how to involve them in the book. One clue to the more 'arty' picture book is that often the illustrations are very sophisticated and adult and

children are very soon bored by them. Good pictures can be looked at again and again and new things found each time. This is as true of good illustration as of all great art.

Race

Multi-ethnic considerations are very important indeed and should not be ignored whatever the particular school situation. Britain is now a racially mixed society and so regardless of where you may live or the mix within a school, all selection should take account of society as a whole and endeavour to reflect that in what is provided in the way of resources. Important areas to watch are the following:

1. Try to avoid books which always have a white hero and where one particular group are always the servants or the underdogs. This is a special problem in stories published either before the last war or just after, and many of these have been reprinted. Look instead for ones which give a positive image of all sorts and types of people. Who makes the decisions and who is the leader?

2. Avoid national stereotyping in books, e.g. the 'stupid Irish' or the 'mean Scot'.

3. History and geography are particular problem areas and often have very eurocentric views. In a book on Africa, for instance, check what it says about pre-colonial days and if it has anything to say about values or life-styles other than European ones. If you inherit a library with much older material in it, then it should be one of your first tasks to check this section and discard inappropriate material.

4. Watch for any illustrations. There has been a school of thought that puts a token black face into the pictures in a book in order to make it 'multi-racial' and so hopefully sell better! This is on the wane now but it still does exist.

5. Culture and lifestyle are very important to everyone and part of all our upbringing. Books should reflect this and give equal value to all the differing sorts.

Gender

Gender is an issue which has become much more important fairly recently and there have been quite a few initiatives to bring this to the attention of the publishing world, the media and people in education.

It is possible to take most of the criteria for multi-ethnic selection, substitute 'female' instead of race and apply those same rules to checking books for gender bias. It certainly was true that many stories had the boys doing all the exciting things whilst the girls made the tea. Teachers and librarians alike need to bear in mind that young children are influenced by the models and roles that they meet in school and by what is offered to them there. Some of the worst examples of books with sex stereotyping have been phased out (reading schemes used to be quite horrendous!) but it is still a salutary experience for any librarian to check their stock and be aware of the issues involved.

Other contentious material

A final area that school librarians must acknowledge and make their own decisions over is the one of possibly contentious material. Over recent years, many topics that previously were hardly even touched on in the adult field are now commonplace in the teenage lists—and sometimes for even younger children—and this may raise problems for the school librarian. The two main areas that need care and thought are in the language used in some books and also in the more explicit sexual content of many books. Many people will feel that this more open approach is a move in the right direction but is has to be recognised that there is substantial criticism within the public as a whole and this could well affect your stance.

Individual circumstances will play a part in whether you feel you can stock such material. Some of the following factors may influence you:

1. What age-ranges does your library serve? If you have the eleven year olds having the same access to all the stock as the sixth form, this could lead to difficulties.
2. Is your library staffed on a full-time basis? This makes it much easier at least to monitor any potentially explosive material.
3. How do other members of staff feel? This is important as if there is, for instance, a parental complaint, then the class teacher may be the one initially in the firing line.
4. It is important to be responsible in selection rather than censorious and to make sure that what you stock does not sensationalise or trivialise relationships, nor use obscene or other unacceptable language unnecessarily.

5. School librarians who can demonstrate a well thought-out, coherent and professional selection policy will not only find the whole task much easier but also will be in a very strong position should criticisms over any resource arise.

CONCLUSIONS

It may seem that the whole business of selection is a full-time job and it certainly does take time, experience and expertise to do it well. However, it is one of the most important, and enjoyable, parts of a librarian's role and should be treated as such. We all spend time worrying over whether children are eating the right food, whether their shoes still fit and when they last had a dental check. It is certainly as important, and many would argue more so, to worry over what goes into their heads and brains. School librarians have a duty to make sure that it is the very best they can offer.

10
New Technology and the Future of School Libraries

What is now called 'new technology' has in many cases been around for a long time, and used in other sorts of libraries over a long period. However, as far as schools are concerned—and some school libraries in particular—then the developments over the last five years or so have been quite dramatic. As computers began to flood into all schools in the early 1980s and various organisations like the Microelectronics Education Programme (MEP) were set up to provide information, in-service training and materials, so school librarians began to consider their own role in this revolution and what it meant in terms of information retrieval, housekeeping functions and especially the skills pupils and other staff would need to develop to make full use of this new potential.

Not surprisingly, it was the professional librarians who were in the forefront of promoting the close liaison between the library and the computer. Even if they had not worked with computers in public or large academic libraries themselves, this would certainly have been an important part of their professional education and all librarians would understand the implications for the library of the computer revolution in education generally.

Teacher-librarians were not so quick to see the links and there are many who still either cannot or do not want to become involved in these moves. Some of this is undoubtedly due to lack of time, some of it to lack of knowledge (not very surprising, particularly as most teacher-librarians are drawn from the English department) and some of it due to a lack of co-operation from other members of staff who may decide that their call on computer time has a higher priority that the library's.

INFORMATION TECHNOLOGY AND SCHOOLS

Information technology has three main elements:

1. The collection, storage and retrieval of information by electronic or mechanical means.
2. The transmission and communication of that information.
3. The manipulation of the information by putting it into different forms for particular purposes.

For school pupils it is the emphasis on information that is the most important and their ability to handle a computerised database with its necessary search routines that is vital. However, the benefits of the computer's ability to communicate that information via a printer or perhaps through a networking system to another school in another area should not be ignored. Likewise, pupils can gain valuable experience and knowledge in manipulating and changing information for their own particular needs. Implicit in this task is the ability to select and evaluate as well as communicate the results in a meaningful fashion.

Too many schools have concentrated on the 'technology' aspect and the hardware without stressing these other areas, but this is not so very surprising as few teachers will have had any training or experience in information retrieval and rarely seen the part computers have long played in the library world. The danger always must be that new technology is seen as an end in itself and not as a means to an end. What emphasis there has been in schools has tended to concentrate on computer science and on CAL (computer-assisted learning).

THE CASE FOR A LIBRARY COMPUTER

Laying the ground work

It is likely that most school librarians will probably have to make a case for a computer and there will probably be a considerable amount of ground work to do first. Some LEAs have already seen the advantages of encouraging the links between computers, information and libraries but for many school librarians that battle still has to be fought. Senior management in some schools may not be aware of, nor receptive to, the concept of a computer as a retrieval or information tool and may even not be convinced of the importance of the whole study and information skills curriculum. School librarians who do not address this probable lack of knowledge and understanding on the part of their colleagues will be unlikely to succeed. Any submission, then, should cover three main areas:

1. An appreciation of the role computers play in information retrieval and handling.
2. The educational arguments for resources and financial provisions to cover the cost of a computer in the library.
3. A plan and proposed syllabus for the integration of the library computer into the curriculum, with details of the benefits to pupils learning strategies and to teaching method. This will carry much more weight if it has been worked out in co-operation with perhaps a subject department or with teachers involved in a particular area of work.

For most schools the library use of computers will probably cover four or five main areas of work, but much will depend on both the age-range of the pupils and on the individual circumstances (not to mention finance!) of each school. Whatever your situation, the following points at least will need consideration:

1. The school library and librarian should already have a high profile and be well used.
2. The school library should be well organised and linked into the teaching. If a case is to be made on the basis of enhancing and extending pupils' skills, it will be much easier to persuade people if this is seen as a development of what already takes place rather than a completely unknown factor.
3. It makes little sense to ask for a computer if there is no time for even the simple routines, never mind the more exploitive and disseminating techniques. Contrary to some amateur opinion, computerised issue systems and similar routine tasks do not save that much staff time, and certainly they are very time-consuming in the early stages when large banks of information must be fed into the software.
4. In addition, it is also not a good idea to include this computerisation of routine library tasks in your arguments as these could well use up much of the available computer capacity and possibly computer time. This could mean the loss of an effective teaching instrument and of any emphasis on information technology.
5. The librarian must have a reasonable knowledge of and be fairly confident in him or herself in this area of work. It would be

preferable to have had experience in information retrieval work but if not that at least to have had some training or in-service courses. There will be computer 'experts' within the school, no doubt, but their expertise will probably be largely irrelevant to the library and be concentrated on either the computer science department or perhaps in using CAL.

6. In view of (5), it is likely that any request for a computer in the library will have to include a fairly detailed explanation of information technology and its growing importance to both pupils and teachers.

7. The librarian must have enough knowledge of computer hardware to be able to assess and suggest the best model for library operations together with any peripherals like printers, modems, etc. Additionally, as there will be other teachers with considerable computer experience on the staff, it is important for the librarian to understand the jargon and be not only able but also confident in discussing the subject.

8. The librarian must also have knowledge of what is available and suitable in the way of software (and in addition how expensive it might be). In this connection it will be necessary to decide how much or how little is to be put into the computer, e.g. a sample database? the issue system? other records?

9. Are other link-ups contemplated with perhaps Prestel or a local network?

10. Making as many visits as possible to school libraries that do have computers and learning from their experience.

Making your case
The main areas that are very important in any submission for a library computer and where the main arguments and emphasis should be concentrated are as follows:

1. *Information retrieval*. This should lie at the heart of any case and the gains to be made both to the curriculum in general and to the study and information skills aspect in particular must be stressed. The fact that pupils will learn to view a computer as a normal part of their search strategy is a gain in itself but, more importantly, they will also develop the techniques vital for successful outcomes. The

search strategies that they must use to access computerised information sources can only complement and enhance the skills learned through print-based enquiries. They will also become competent not only at the loading and unloading of software but also in keyboarding skills. The ability to define and articulate their information needs is enhanced by using computerised databases and their growing confidence when using 'key words' or similiar 'concept' indexing terms is a skill that can be transferred to any medium. School programs can be directly related to pupil needs in a way that is difficult if not impossible with other information sources and this facility means that the cycle of selecting, processing and communication information can be much more controlled so that specific educational and learning outcomes can be built in.

2. *Word processing.* This is worth its weight in gold for staff and students alike. It can save hours of staff time in preparing lesson material, standard letters or routine forms. Pupils can learn how to set out different sorts of written communication, experiment with different styles of print and gain valuable computer experience whilst so doing. The library, in particular, can benefit by being able to produce overdue notices or similiar stationery quickly and cheaply.

3. *Providing access to other databases.* The computer could be used to communicate with other computers or access databases such as Prestel, or perhaps the school could join a locally established network. A useful facility of Prestel and similiar databases is that programs can be loaded from them onto disc and used off-line thereby incurring no further charges. *The Times Network for Schools* allows schools throughout the country to communicate with a large mainframe computer that holds a large amount of information.

4. *'In-house' databases.* These can be specifically built up to respond to a known need within the school, such as careers information or a special subject file. There are now some good software packages for careers information and they can be particularly useful for older pupils.

5. *Program bank.* A 'software library' of programs, either commercially produced or written within the school, can be built up, including CAL material as well as other topics. The programs in such a library could be borrowed by staff and pupils alike. This can be

a most important use of the library computer from an educational point of view, allowing not only a range of material to be provided but also encouraging all pupils in the school, regardless of ability or subject option, to gain valuable experience and expertise in computer operation. There is also usually help available in the library both in how to operate the hardware and in how to select appropriate programs.

To provide as full a range of computer services as possible, the library should really have a computer with disc drive, preferably a dual one to give greater flexibility. Disc is so much faster than tape and has increasingly superseded tape, although some smaller schools in the primary sector may still not be able to afford the more sophisticated equipment. A printer that can give high quality results as well as a variety of typefaces will be needed, as will a monitor that can cope with colour (quite a substantial number of commercial software programs use colour) and, of course, the discs, paper and software necessary to operate the system. All this will not be cheap so this makes it even more imperative that the librarian's case for this investment is carefully presented and fully researched. If links with either Prestel or other networks are envisaged, then more costs for the installation of a modem will be incurred, although the benefits to the school and pupils of this additional facility could be great. Some of this expense will be a 'one-off' capital amount to buy the initial hardware, but provision will have to be made on an annual basis for stationery, telephone bills if Prestel or other external bases are accessed as well as for buying new programs or updating the equipment.

Some school libraries, in the interests of economy and probably because they could see no other alternative, have compromised and made use of computers that are actually housed in other school departments. Although this may be marginally better than nothing, it is not very satisfactory either for the library staff concerned or for other potential users. Fitting in library use with other lessons is very difficult, access is restricted and effective development unlikely. Once having accepted such a compromise it may be all the more difficult to press for a library-based facility. Press, always, for the library to have its own computer with the school librarian in charge of its operation. Remember to stress:

1. Your case for a computer worked out in co-operation with teaching colleagues.
2. The educational rationale for such a move.
3. The professionalism both of your knowledge and understanding and also in the way you present the report.

CONCLUSIONS

As more and more information is held on computer databases and they become an everyday part of most people's lives, then all schools must ensure that their pupils have the necessary skills, both technical and evaluative, to access these with confidence. In 1980, an American, Daniel Watt, talking at a National Science Foundation Conference, said: 'A society ceases to be functionally democratic when decision-making must be left in the hands of an influential minority with technical expertise and economic power, or when it is indeed exercised by the population at large if that population cannot make informed judgements about crucial matters.' It is a warning of what could happen if all school librarians do not respond to the challenge of the new technology and give all pupils this expertise.

What, then, is the future for school librarians and their libraries in the country as a whole? As this book has attempted to show, there always has been, and still is, a great discrepancy in provision from one LEA to another, and although it would be simplistic to put it all down to the North – South divide, certainly it is amongst the more affluent southern areas that services of a very high standard are more the norm. However, glimmerings of a more national concern can be seen and both the School Library Association and the Library Association are using their power bases to more effective use than at possibly any other time before. Representations are made to Ministers, meetings with the decision-makers arranged and a much higher profile altogether given to the importance of information skills for both pupils and their teachers, together with the essential part that librarians play in this process.

Some of the impetus for this has undoubtedly come from the introduction of the GCSE syllabus. This has helped to provide a climate in which school librarians are more readily heard and their skills are more fully acknowledged. There are still great problems ahead, most of them to do with staffing and funding, and until these can be resolved there is little point in pretending that a school library can operate on any sort of effective basis.

The question of qualifications for school librarians is still simmering and has never been resolved on any national basis, although some individual authorities have produced their own policies. Others are still anything up to fifty years behind and their 'standard' of provision is abysmal. Access to training and possible dual qualification is a part of this dilemma but again, the lack of any national initiative, particularly for teachers wishing to obtain some basic library skills, has exacerbated the situation.

Not all is doom and gloom, though. More posts are being advertised for school librarians, many more publications are now on the market and much more is heard in education generally about the role of the school librarian. Given the present economic climate, it will not be easy for all school libraries to play their rightful part, but at least now there is a more general acknowledgement of their importance to all pupils and of the essential and unique qualities that the school librarian brings to education. An HMI is reputed to have said that school libraries should be 'powerhouses not poorhouses'. That must be the maxim for the future.

Bibliography

1. Beswick, N. (Summer 1983) The controversial school library. *Education Libraries Bulletin,* **26** (2), pp. 1 – 15.
2. Beswick, N. (Summer 1986) Is it school librarianship? *International Review of Children's Literature and Librarianship,* **1** (2), pp. 1 – 11.
3. Davies, R.E. (1979) *The School Library: A Force for Educational Change,* Bowker.
4. *Dewey Decimal Classification: An Introduction for British Schools,* revised and expanded by Mary L. South (available from Don Gresswell, Bridge House, Grange Park, London N21 1RB).
5. Furlong, N. and Platt, P. (1984) *Cataloguing Rules for Books and Other Media in Primary and Secondary Schools,* 6th edition, School Library Association.
6. Gordon, C. (1986) *Resource Organisation in Primary Schools,* Council for Educational Technology.
7. Haycock, K. (Summer 1985) Strengthening the foundations of teacher-librarianship. *Education Libraries Bulletin,* **28** (2), pp. 11 – 22.
8. Herring, J. (1987) *The Microcomputer, the School Librarian and the Teacher,* Bingley.
9. *Information Technology and the School Library Resource Centre* (1983) Microelectronics Education Programme and the Library Association.
10. *Information Skills in the Secondary Curriculum* (1983) Schools Council Bulletin No. 9, Methuen.
11. Irving, A. (1982) *Starting to Teach Study Skills,* Arnold.
12. King, E.J. (1987) *How to Use a Library,* Northcote House.
13. King, E.J. (Summer 1987) The School Library Association of Great Britain: its first fifty years. *International Review of Children's Literature and Librarianship,* **2** (2), pp. 82 – 94.
14. *Library Association (1977) Library Resource Provision in Schools: Guidelines and Recommendations,* Library Association.

15. McDonald, M.M. (1985) *Towards Excellence: Case Studies of Good School Libraries,* Library Association.
16. Pain, H. and Lesquereux, J. (1985) *Studies in School Library Management 1: Developing a Policy for the School Library,* School Libraries Group.
17. Pain, H. and Lesquereux, J. (1986) *Studies in School Library Management 2: Implementing the School Library Policy,* School Libraries Group.
18. School Library Association (1980) *The Way Ahead: The Organisation and Staffing of Resources in Schools in the 1980s,* School Library Association.
19. *School Libraries: The Foundations of the Curriculum* (1984) Library Information Series No. 13, HMSO
20. *Secondary School Library Survey* (1981) Statistical Bulletin 7/81, HMSO.
21. *Special Educational Needs* (1978) Report of the Committee of Enquiry into the Education of Handicapped Children and Young People, HMSO.
22. *A Survey of Secondary School Libraries in Six Local Education Authorities* (1985) HMSO.
23. Thomson, L. and Meek, M. (undated) *Developing Resource-Based Learning, Longman Resources Unit.*

Index